THE CARNEGIE
LIBRARY OF
PITTSBURGH

Music & Art Department

Where's the Melody?

A Listener's Introduction to Jazz

by

MARTIN T. WILLIAMS

A DA CAPO PAPERBACK

Library of Congress Cataloging in Publication Data

Williams, Martin T.
  Where's the melody?

  (A Da Capo paperback)
  Reprint. Originally published: 1st ed. New York: Pantheon Books,
© 1966.
  Discography: p.
  1. Jazz music — History and criticism.   2. Jazz music — Discography.
I. Title.
[ML3506.W547 1983]   781′.57   82-23644
ISBN 0-306-80183-3 (pbk.)

Acknowledgments

Portions of this book have appeared in slightly different form in the
Saturday Review, in editor Irving Kolodin's "Recordings" section; in
Down Beat ("Monk at the Five Spot," "Recording with 'Bags,'" and
"Giuffre at Home"); in *Evergreen Review*; and in *Harper's
Magazine*. I would like to thank the Saturday Review, Inc., *Down
Beat* and its editor Don DeMicheal, Grove Press and *Evergreen
Review*, and *Harper's* for permission to use that material here.
And special thanks go to Paula McGuire of Pantheon Books, for
this book was her idea.
M.W.

This Da Capo Press paperback edition of *Where's the Melody! A
Listener's Introduction to Jazz* is an unabridged republication of
the first edition published in New York in 1966, supplemented
with a note on discography references. It is reprinted by arrangement with the author.

Published by Da Capo Press, Inc.
A Subsidiary of Plenum Publishing Corporation
233 Spring Street, New York, N.Y. 10013

A NOTE ON THE
DISCOGRAPHY REFERENCES
IN THE DA CAPO EDITION

Where's the Melody? was revised in 1969 and it is that version which the reader now has in hand. By then several of the discographical references in the original edition were out of date—recordings had passed out of the catalogue or individual selections had appeared in different collations or LP collections. The book's editors and author decided, however, to leave those references as they had originally appeared—they would give the reader no real problems—and attend to revisions that seemed more important. For one thing, if we had re-listed recordings by their then-current or most recently available catalogue numbers and labels, these listings might in turn have gone out of print by the time the volume reached its readers.

We have made the same decision for the Da Capo edition. Phonograph records go in and out of print, in and out of collations, even back and forth from one label to another, with a dizzying frequency. One is no sooner unable to locate a classic title on a domestic LP, and decides the collection has gone out of the catalogue, than the performance reappears in a new collection from France or Italy, or in an exact replica of its original release, jacket design and all, from Japan.

Rather than try to ride out such a rapid flow and flux, we have decided to put the reader somewhat on his own. The references herein will serve to identify the records under discussion, and also to identify specific versions of often-recorded pieces as well. As the text makes clear, we describe Count Basie's *One O'clock Jump* in its original version, recorded for Decca; and Benny Goodman's frequently recorded *Sometimes I'm Happy* in its 1935 Victor interpretation.

The reader should have no more difficulty in dealing with these listings than he might have with somewhat more updated, but no more reliably current references. And in a well-stocked record shop, with the help of a sympathetic clerk, he should have very little trouble. He may even enjoy the quest.

—MARTIN WILLIAMS
Washington, D.C.
January, 1983

CONTENTS

INTRODUCTION:
"An American Art"

If we know anything about jazz at all, we have probably heard that it is supposed to be an art—our only art according to some; "America's contribution to the arts," according to certain European commentators. It has also the kind of prestige that goes with praise from the "classical" side of the fence. One of the first men to recognize the artistic qualities of jazz was the outstanding Swiss conductor Ernest Ansermet, who in 1919 wrote a tribute to the great clarinetist and soprano saxophonist Sidney Bechet, adding that perhaps tomorrow the whole world would be moving along his road. And in 1965 the American composer-critic Virgil Thomson said that "jazz is the most astounding spontaneous musical event to take place anywhere since the Reformation."

Jazz has its special publications, both here and abroad, its own journalists, reviewers, critics, historians, and scholars. Also, as most of us are aware, our State Department is willing to export jazz to answer for our cultural prestige abroad. Yet here at home, this "American art" is the subject of certain ignorance and certain misunderstandings.

It is possible to approach jazz in several ways. It is more than possible—it is in a sense almost mandatory—to consider jazz as an aspect of Negro American life and of the far-reaching and little understood effect of Negro-American life on American life in general. Jazz is, of course, a product of Negro-American culture, and that means that it represents also a unique coming together of African and European musical traditions.

It is also possible to treat jazz at second hand, as it has influenced our other music. The results of this approach might surprise some of us, for there is hardly a corner of American music that has not been touched somehow by jazz. It has touched most corners of music in Europe as well. To give one rather unexpected example, most of the trumpet players in our symphony orchestras, whether they are performing Bach or Bartok, Grieg or Gershwin, play with a slight *vibrato* (literally, a vibration to their trumpet sound) that they are not supposed to have, because in the past jazz musicians have generally used one. The symphonists have simply picked it up, some of them perhaps unconsciously.

It is not surprising that all American popular

music, and some American concert music as well, were once commonly referred to as "jazz," because the influence of jazz and of pre-jazz Afro-American music is everywhere in our musical life—on Broadway, in musical films, in the hotel dance band, in the "hit parade," in the concert hall. And, in one form or another, this influence has been there for over seventy years. So apparently "square" a popular song as *Dancing in the Dark* would not have been written without the powerful and pervasive effect of the musical force we call "jazz."

Jazz has also been treated through the biographies of its players, and some writers have treated jazzmen as what they are—creative people, most often functioning as popular entertainers. But jazzmen have also been treated as colorful old characters or as pathetic, aging men, unworthy of the callous caprice with which a delinquent showbiz has shunted them aside. It is possible, after all, for the most interesting of men, or even the most colorful of old characters, to be involved in an activity that need not detain us for its own sake. We might appreciate the personal maturity of a shop steward without being interested in owning a handbook on union organization at the local level or one on the processing of auto parts on a modern assembly line.

However, jazz is a music, and it is worthy of our attention as a music. Its musical achievements are quite high, perhaps higher than those of any other so-called "folk" or "popular" music in human history. Undoubtedly the musical level of jazz would have had to be high before it could have exerted such a strong and continuing influence upon other musics. But jazz music itself is much more interesting than the subject of its influence. It has a life of its own, growing, developing, and finding its own way, taking what it needs from the European tradition and adding something of its own at each step. And, as the years pass, jazz behaves less and less like a "popular" commercial music, subject to the fads of the moment, and more and more like what we are apt to think of (rightly or wrongly) as an "art music."

Let us assume in looking at jazz that we know little or nothing about the techniques of music and little or nothing about jazz and its history.

We will assume we know little about jazz history because we want to look at it from a musical standpoint, and because very little that we can appreciate has been written on it from that standpoint. And we will assume that we don't know much about music, because many of us don't. But perhaps lack of a detailed musical background is an advantage. Jazz has taught itself, so to speak. Jazz musicians have often taught themselves and the music as a whole has wended its selective way, almost on its own, through the techniques of European music. If we were to study music, we would of course study a system largely deduced from practice, a theory derived from what the great European composers have actually done when they wrote. But sometimes this musical system and theory applies to jazz only approximately, only insofar as jazz musicians have borrowed it, transmuted it, and used it in their own way. So, in listening to a partly self-taught music, we shall probably have the gods on our side if we become self-taught listeners.

We do not learn to listen theoretically or in the abstract, of course, and almost all the comments in this book are attached to specific recordings. We shall begin by going directly to the crux of the matter, to the jazz musician as he plays combinations and sequences of notes that sound sometimes familiar, sometimes only vaguely familiar, and sometimes not familiar at all. And we shall try to understand how jazz musicians play, what they do with a melody; how much they improvise, make up as they go along, and how much they work out ahead of time; and the kind of musical logic involved in their way of playing.

There is, after all, little point in worrying about the history of an art or the biographies of its players until we have some familiarity with the art itself. As an introduction to how jazz players play, we will look in the first section of this book, "Where's the Melody?" at what they do with more or less familiar popular songs. Then we will turn to an important original musical form that has been used by jazzmen of all styles and periods, the form called "the Blues." With these basic forms and practices in mind, we can examine "Eight Recorded Solos" in more careful detail.

Having been thus introduced to the work of the jazz soloist, we can turn, in the section called "What Does a Composer Do?" to the jazz composer-arranger, the man who provides the player with basic material or who revises material he finds in the American popular repertory. The composer-arranger orchestrates; he gives the musicians in large and small ensembles written (or sometimes memorized) parts to play and he assigns the soloists space and duration in which to improvise. A soloist is responsible for his portion of a performance; a composer-arranger for the effect of the whole.

In these four introductory sections we have deliberately avoided chronology and avoided the sometimes careless catch-phrases of styles and schools and periods of jazz. The things that Louis Armstrong and Thelonious Monk have in common as players are more important and instructive than differences in the way they make music. Teddy Wilson, a pianist who first rose to prominence in the mid-Thirties, in those days took the same basic approach to improvised invention as did Charlie Parker, the revolutionary figure of the mid-Forties. And the music of the pianist and leader from the "swing period," Count Basie, taught the modernist John Lewis as much as did Charlie Parker's music—perhaps more.

Having examined the basics of jazz this far, we are now in a position to look at its musical history in "Last Trip Up the River." From a musical standpoint that history is made up of the contributions of certain major jazz players who renew the basic language of the music periodically, men like Louis Armstrong and Charlie Parker, and of certain major jazz composers, men like Duke Ellington, who periodically give larger synthesis and summary and form to the music.

After paying this much attention to the music itself, it is perhaps time to have accounts of the players at work on the scene—in nightclubs, in studios, and in private rehearsals. Thus, the second part of this book describes a nightclub evening of a pianist-composer, "Monk at the Five Spot"; a record date by vibraharpist Milt Jackson and a brass ensemble, "Recording with 'Bags'"; another recording session by a Mississippi blues singer of the old school, "Big Joe in the Studio"; and a rehearsal by some of the men who are involved in the avant-garde with "Jimmy Giuffre at Home."

The final part of this book, "Comment by a Listener," represents an effort to return to the music and its musicians with the knowledge so far acquired. In comments (some brief and some more comprehensive) on figures like Horace Silver, Billie Holiday, and Roy Eldridge, I have expanded on some of the points of jazz history described in the first part of the book and have tried to show, in a more or less casual sampling, how some exceptional musicians have developed the ideas of the great figures and have also made contributions of their own. I have also dealt with the work of some less creative figures who water down and popularize the musical ideas of others. I have used as examples some recorded performances which do not seem to me successful; the value in this is not in point-ing the finger at failure (or my idea of failure) but rather in discussing how and why performances may fail. Finally, I have commented on recent develop-ments and the jazz avant-garde as exemplified by Ornette Coleman.

I have not tried in this book to disguise my enthu-siasm for jazz and for most of the players and perform-ers I have discussed. But I have tried not to include too many of my own specific emotional responses to the musicians and their work. My purpose in this book has been to clear the way, to help listeners discover their own responses by putting them more directly in touch with the music itself. I have suggested my own feelings about jazz, I trust, largely as a means to such an end.

Finally, I think that each reader should undertake a book of this sort at his own pace—even at his own leisure—and that for some a gradual alternation of reading and listening can be the most rewarding. With that purpose in mind, I have included suggestions for a "Basic Library of Jazz" and have, in various sections, added "Record Notes" which list representative works of the artists discussed. The reader will, I hope, take it from there.

ON THE MUSIC

Where's the Melody?

Let us assume that we are following two men as they enter a jazz nightclub or arrive, a few minutes late, at a jazz concert. One of them is an avid fan, an insider who has been following the music enthusiastically for years. His friend is not an insider; he is curious and sympathetic but a little puzzled. As they move inside the club or concert hall, the music is underway. The novice turns to the insider and asks, "What are they playing, do you know?"

The master replies, "That's A *Foggy Day*."

At this point we can discern puzzlement, and perhaps despair, on the face of our novice. He knows perfectly well what A *Foggy Day in London Town* sounds like, and he hears nothing whatever like its melody coming from the musicians in front of him. Yet his friend is sure that it's A *Foggy Day*. Jazz must be some kind of musical puzzle.

In effect, our novice has asked a prevelant question, "Where's the melody?" Or, to put it more crudely, "What are those musicians *doing* up there?" It is a question that is considered so square by some jazz fans, and even some musicians, that they refuse to answer—or even hear it. Yet I think it is a perfectly valid question, and answering it can be enlightening. For what those musicians are "doing up there" is not very obscure. It is not wholly unprecedented in the Western European music from which American music partly derives. And it is certainly no kind of musical game or puzzle.

Most of us probably know that jazz musicians make variations on a theme and that these variations are often improvised, invented on the spot as they play. For many people the primary quality in jazz is its rhythm—jazz is a particular rhythmic way of playing music. And anyone who has ever watched a group of jazz fans will be led to suspect that more than a few of them are responding to jazz rhythm—and very little else. There is nothing invalid about such a response, for its particular way of handling rhythm is indeed one of the unique things and one of the most compelling things about jazz music. But on the other hand, jazz rhythm, on the surface at least, is a readily recognizable quality. For our novice it is probably the thing that for him makes jazz jazz. He hears it, he feels it, and he says, "That's jazz." He may not always be right and he may not sense the fine details of whether the musicians are handling jazz rhythms well (that is, whether they are "swinging"), but he will be right most of the time.

Let's take a familiar popular song, which is what jazz-men do about half the time. There is nothing in the popular song that necessarily makes it jazz. It may have been influenced by jazz, even heavily influenced, as most American popular music has. But if a jazz musician plays it, he will play it with jazz rhythm. He will make it "swing," give it a particular kind of momentum and movement. Thus, a jazz musician has already made a *rhythmic* variation on a piece by performing it at all. But so far he has given us no problems, for he has used the familiar melody in a recognizable way— let us say it is *A Foggy Day* or *Pennies from Heaven* or *Embraceable You* or any of thousands of American popular songs that are familiar to most of us and that are commonly used by jazz musicians.

Almost any jazz performance of familiar pieces like those will have at least an opening chorus based on the familiar melody itself. However, many jazz musicians use the melody not just for their opening statements, but as a basis of everything they do. There are players from every style and school of jazz who play that way; if you came in in the middle of one of their performances you would probably know right away what they were playing.

But such performances are not a matter of playing the same thing over and over again. These players make variations. For example, they will embellish the melody in various ways: they will add decorative notes and phrases, they will fill in in places where the melody comes to rest, and they will make slight changes in the notes as written.

At the same time they may improvise with the harmony of a piece (particularly if they are pianists), altering the simple chords that you and I would find on a piece of sheet music and even adding other chords.

Now, of course, these things can be done badly. Some decorations can be cluttering and affected. The point of the melodic embellishments and of the richer harmony is to enhance the piece, to bring out its good qualities or modify its poor ones, and, at best, to discover hidden qualities and make a better piece of music of it. The great master of this particular embellishment approach to jazz improvising was the pianist Art Tatum whose additions and fills were often dazzling, and whose sense of rich, improvised harmony was probably the most developed that our popular music has ever seen.

But besides filling out and elaborating the melody, a jazz musician can subtract from it, can reduce it to a kind of outline, and can come up with fascinating musical experience thereby. Thelonious Monk, because of his exceptional and subtle sense of rhythm, can take even a silly popular ditty and make it sound like a first-rate composition for piano—his version of *You Took the Words Right Out of My Heart* is a good example, or, to take a better song, his rephrasing of *I Should Care*.

Another player who uses this melodic approach to variations is Erroll Garner. And there are horn players, particularly from older generations, who are excellent at this kind of paraphrase of familiar melodies.

The greatest of all is Louis Armstrong, who can work with good popular material like *I Gotta Right to Sing the Blues* and improve it, or who can work with poor material like *That's My Home* and make it sound like deathless melody.

Thus a great deal of jazz variation is recognizably made on a familiar melody, and there are players from all styles and schools who use this approach. They may elaborate the melody, they may decorate it, or they may reduce it and simplify it (basically, these are what a classicist would call kinds of "melodic variation"), and they may re-harmonize it. But it is always there somewhere. The art lies in how well they transmute it, in how good a paraphrase they come up with while transforming what is written.

Now let's go back to our jazz fan and his novice friend who were entering the club or concert. Let's assume that now they are comfortably in their seats, that the Miles Davis ensemble is performing, and that they begin *Bye Bye, Blackbird*. In the first chorus of this piece our novice would hear a transmutation of a familiar, perhaps appealing, but obviously and deliberately lightweight popular ditty from the Twenties. He will realize that there is indeed a sea change taking place, however, for although Davis' trumpet is keeping recognizably to the written melody, he has transformed it, making it a kind of buoyant dirge. Then, in Davis' second chorus, there suddenly seems to be no more *Bye Bye, Blackbird*. What is going on?

What is going on is that Miles Davis is offering a new melody, one which he is improvising on the spot.

This melody does continue the mood and the musical implications he was sketching in his first chorus, but it offers some very new ideas of melody.

Davis is using as his guide for this new melody what we may call an "outline" or "framework" of *Bye Bye, Blackbird*. Technically speaking, he is using what musicians call the "chord changes," the harmonic understructure, of *Bye Bye, Blackbird* as the basis for this melody of his own. (Classicists would call this a harmonic variation, incidentally.)

The way to listen to him now is to listen not for something we already know or have already heard, but for the music that Miles Davis is making *as we hear him*. If we also hear, or sense unconsciously, that "outline," that related chord structure the player is using as his guide, fine. But we don't have to. Jazz is not a musical game or puzzle.

Sometimes jazz musicians will use a familiar structure, a familiar set of chord changes from a standard popular song, *without* using the theme melody at all, even for their opening chorus. They simply invent, from the very beginning, without any theme statement or paraphrase. Classic examples are Lester Young's 1944 version of *These Foolish Things* and Charlie Parker's *Embraceable You*. In each case the player is using the familiar harmonic outline for *his* guide—but not necessarily for *ours*. Again, jazz variation is not a guessing game or a puzzle. Where's the melody? Well, again, the melody is the one that Lester Young or Charlie Parker is making up, the one he is playing. It is not something we have heard before; it may even seem to be like nothing we have heard before. It is what he is playing. Hear it, enjoy it. And hear it well, for it may not exist again.

Similarly, jazz musicians sometimes introduce their improvising with new themes, written or memorized, which are also patterned to old chord structures. Thus, *Ornithology* takes its outline from *How High the Moon*; Count Basie's *Roseland Shuffle* came from *Shoeshine Boy*; *Moten Swing* came from *You're Drivin' Me Crazy*; and there are probably at least two thousand jazz originals, from Sidney Bechet's *Shag* through Ornette Coleman's *Angel Voice*, based on the chords to Gershwin's *I Got Rhythm*. An obvious reason for this is that the new themes have a more jazzlike melodic character than the popular songs which were their harmonic origin.

Thus there are three kinds of variations—those that involve rhythm, which are intrinsic in jazz performances, as we have seen; those that involve embellishing or paraphrasing a written melody, either decorating it or subtracting from it or both; and those that involve the invention of new melodies within a harmonic outline. They are all found, alone or more often in combination, in all styles and schools of jazz except the most recent.

At this point, let's try a summary by example. Let us assume that we play a little bit of piano and read a little bit of music. We are attracted to a particular popular song and purchase a piece of sheet music for that song to try it out on the parlor spinet. The sheet music will probably present the song in a fairly simple manner. The right-hand piano part, the treble, will give its melody. The left-hand part, the bass, will give simple chords that fit that melody; usually the chords given on sheet music are simple, and often they are quite simple. We take the piece home and play it over a few times until we've got it, as written down, fairly smoothly.

For most people this is the end of the matter. They have learned to play the song as the sheet music presents it. But let us assume that there is a jazz musician inside us and he takes over. The first step would be to play the piece with jazz rhythm. Automatically, this will mean at least some changes in the values of the notes and some personal interpretations of the accents. We have begun to make the piece "swing." Actually, an authentic "swing" is not an easy matter, but let's assume we're getting one fairly well.

Incidentally, in doing this we have discovered that making a piece of music "swing" has nothing to do with playing it fast or loud. It is a matter of giving it a particular kind of rhythm. It can be done slowly and quietly. (Actually, it is very difficult to swing at extremely slow tempo or at extremely fast tempo—but that technicality needn't detain us now.) *

---

* The word "swing" is obviously a part of the technical vocabulary of jazz music. It is a quality empirically present or not present in a performance, and the particular rhythmic momentum of "swing" can be felt and heard. However, the term has never been satisfactorily defined. Perhaps the best description is one critic's phrase "getting the notes in the right place"—that is, in the right place with relationship to

Now let's say that under the impetus of that swing and its unique momentum, we begin to try changing certain of the melody notes more boldly. What we have already changed suggests more changes, and we extend some, we shorten others, we leave out some, we add others. We begin to get a different piece of music. At the same time, perhaps we hear more interesting harmonies for the left hand. We change a few of the chords to make them richer, and, in passing, we perhaps add a few appropriate tones that weren't there.

Now, the final step: suppose we gradually diminish the original right-hand part—the treble, the melody notes—altogether. We keep the left-hand part (or our version of it) and with the right hand we make up a new melody part that fits that left-hand part.

It used to be said that modern jazzmen, of the generation of the Forties, began the business of writing new themes to old structures and of inventing new

---

each other and with relationship to the accompaniment that a soloist usually gets. Also, composer Bill Mathieu has suggested that as jazz has evolved, the basic rhythm has tended more and more to center on the string bass (plucked in jazz rather than bowed, as a rule) and the drummer's cymbal because there is a slight delay between the time these instruments are struck and the time they actually sound, and that this delay is essential to the rhythmic character of jazz.

The term "swing" came in with Louis Armstrong's music and was the musicians' word for his particular rhythmic contribution to jazz, but both the rhythm and the term have been retained. Similarly, it is possible to play pre-Armstrong

solo melodies to chords alone. But this is obviously untrue. It is untrue of the blues form, as we shall see. Furthermore, our example of *Moten Swing* comes from 1932, and there are earlier examples of jazz originals with their chords borrowed from, let's say, *After You've Gone*, or *I Ain't Got Nobody*, or *Sweet Sue*, or a dozen others. And, almost all of the great players of the late Thirties—men like pianist Teddy Wilson; tenor saxophonists Coleman Hawkins, Ben Webster, and Lester Young; alto saxophonists Johnny Hodges and Benny Carter; guitarist Charlie Christian —did much of their playing on chord structures alone, with little or no reference to a theme. Indeed, even earlier players were capable of it, and there are many recorded examples of "nonthematic" variations, of variations that invent original melodies, by Bix Beiderbecke, Louis Armstrong, Earl Hines, Jack Teagarden, Sidney Bechet, and even by Bunk Johnson whose style dates from the early days of New Orleans jazz.

Only the youngest players have broken away from using either the melody of a piece or its chords as direct guides for making their solos.

A good paraphrase of a melody by a good jazz musician is frequently quite superior to its point of

---

styles both with and without an appropriate rhythmic character, and the term "swing" has been borrowed and applied to early jazz and even to ragtime. As we began by saying, it is better to hear and feel swing than to attempt to define it, and in the final section of this book, "Comment by a Listener" we shall have some examples of players and performances that do and do not swing.

departure, the original popular song in the standard repertory. And a good melodic invention by a great jazz musician is a piece of spontaneous composition that may be miles ahead of its point of departure. I would not denigrate George Gershwin's achievements; he was one of our best popular composers—indeed, one of our best musicians. But Gershwin was usually writing *songs*, fairly simple melodies intended to be sung, usually by relatively untrained voices. And Charlie Parker's recorded variations on Gershwin's *Embraceable You* and *Lady Be Good* are instrumentally brilliant in a way that Gershwin's songs are not and were not intended to be.

However, Parker, like most great jazzmen, was also a melodist. He was a great *instrumental* melodist when judged by quite exacting musical standards. When we remember that Parker (again, like most great jazzmen) was a player and did his "composing" as he played, by improvisation, then we realize how astonishing his achievement was.

And so, we come back again to our question and our answer. Where's the melody? The melody is the one the player is making. Hear it well, for it probably will not exist again. And it may well be extraordinary.

RECORD NOTES

The great master of embellishment in jazz history was the pianist Art Tatum. Tatum also had one of the great harmonic imaginations—one of the richest left hands—in recorded jazz. There are some who feel that his work was sometimes overdecorative, but getting acquainted with Tatum is a superb introduction to an embellishment style in jazz. The best Tatum available is probably a two-LP album, *"The Real Art Tatum,"* recorded at a party, issued on 20th Century-Fox Records TFM 3162-3. The pianist deals with such familiar pieces as *My Heart Stood Still, September Song, I Cover the Waterfront, Willow Weep for Me, Too Marvelous for Words,* and *Body and Soul.*

Almost the opposite of Tatum's approach to variations based on a theme melody is that of Thelonious Monk. Monk is apt to subtract from the melody as effectively as Tatum adds to it. We listen to Monk for unexpected rhythms and a fascinatingly original piano sound. Unfortunately, two of his best collections of variations on standards are now out of print. These were *"Thelonious Himself"* (Riverside 12-235), which includes *I Should Care,* and *"Thelonious Alone in San Francisco"* (Riverside 12-312), which has *You Took the Words Right Out of My Heart.* They may still be found in some shops. A later Monk solo recital is on Columbia CL 2349; it includes a remake of *I Should Care* which is not up to the original, but well worth hearing. Any good Monk collection will probably have a piano solo piece. There is, for example, *Memories of You* on *"It's Monk's Time"* (Columbia CL 2186) with its fine, humorous, quasi-amateurish effects, and its abstractions of older jazz styles.

Essential Erroll Garner is still Columbia's *"Concert by the Sea"* (CL 883).

Our Armstrong selections come from RCA Victor LPM 2322. Armstrong's accompaniments are notoriously bad on the majority of his recordings, but never mind.

Miles Davis has recorded *Bye Bye, Blackbird* a couple of times. As a beginning, try the one on Columbia CL 949. Once that is familiar, hearing the different one on Columbia CL 1694 can be quite enlightening.

Lester Young's *These Foolish Things* was last issued on Imperial 9181.

Charlie Parker's *Embraceable You* is current on two LPs, Roost 2210 and Parker PLP 407. His *Lady Be Good* solo is in the Verve series *"The Charlie Parker Story"* (8000–8002), a cross-section of Parker's work for that label.

The Blues

As we have seen, jazzmen use several approaches to variation. Where did they come from?

They are more or less analogous to procedures that have been used in European music for several centuries, approaches classicists call rhythmic variation, melodic variation, and harmonic variation. Jazz musicians rediscovered the procedures in their own terms. Afro-American music began to borrow from the European harmonic system well over seventy years ago and has continued to borrow since, adapting that system to its own ends. From that borrowing it was perhaps inevitable that the various approaches to classical variation, or something very close to them, would develop in jazz.

I think we can see that, as jazz musicians became more and more adept at embellishing or decorating a melody, and at the same time more and more adept at subtracting from melody and abstracting it, these additions and subtractions would tend to take over and the original melody would tend more and more to disappear. The player would be aware that he was putting something in the place of the original, of course, and, if he was a good player, he would be aware of the quality of the melody he was providing. Perhaps that is the way the various kinds of jazz variations evolved, at least in part.

At the same time, there was in the jazz tradition a precedent for retaining a harmonic outline and inventing a new melody to fit it. It was common practice in the musical form called "the blues." The blues form is original with Afro-American music and jazz. It does not seem to have had any direct origin in European music, "folk" or "fine." And, despite some interesting analogies and influences from African and Arabic music, the blues form seems to have grown up here in the United States. The blues is obviously a story in itself, and an important one for all kinds of indigenous American music.

We have all probably heard several of the following pieces in the American popular repertory—some vocal, some instrumental, some both: *One O'Clock Jump, Sent for You Yesterday and Here You Come Today, Woodchopper's Ball, It Must Be Jelly, Why Don't You Do Right?*, or, if the reader is a bit younger, *Roll Over Beethoven, You Ain't Nothing But a Hound Dog* or *Ball and Chain*. Actually, these pieces are all in the blues form, all in various versions of the most common kind of blues, which, in musical measure (in the way music is counted off) is very brief—only twelve bars, twelve measures of music per chorus.

Up to now we have discussed jazz based on familiar popular songs, pieces written in a form which comes from Europe and which, incidentally, is usually thirty-two measures of music. But much jazz improvising—and a great deal of other popular music—is in the indigenous American form, the blues. The blues is even found in our so-called "country and western" music, and the blues accounts for many of our rock-and-roll songs.

At this point we should note that music in the blues form covers many moods and is not restricted to "sad songs" done slowly. Similarly, many "sad songs" (like, say, *The Man I Love*) which are often referred to as "blues" are not blues. And many songs with *blues* in their titles are not necessarily true blues. W. C. Handy's *St. Louis Blues* is a blues, but *I Get the Blues When It Rains* is not. The blues, then, is a musical form which can be put to many uses—just as the sonnet is a verse form which can be used for a variety of poetic expressions.

There is indeed much confusion about what is and what isn't blues in American music. When the great jazz singer Billie Holiday died, many journalists described her as "a blues singer." Actually, Miss Holiday had only about four blues in her repertory, and one of those was the *St. Louis Blues*, which practically everyone sings and which therefore doesn't really count. On the other hand, her work was permeated with musical devices and emotional attitudes which do come from the blues, so perhaps there is some justice in the description. Similarly, Pearl Bailey, who has probably sung fewer blues than Billie Holiday, has been described as a blues singer. So, for that matter, has Libby Holman, who is a singer of sentimental and somewhat self-indulgent, carrying-the-torch songs.

Actually, the jazz repertory itself is not altogether free from such confusions. The piece called *Wolverine Blues* by Ferdinand "Jelly Roll" Morton is not actually a blues, although someone (perhaps a song publisher's assistant interested in cashing in on a fad) named it a blues. Neither is the dixieland standard *Jazz Me Blues* a real blues; *Rock Around the Clock*, on the other hand, is.

Most of us know the blues in its vocal version—a line of verse (roughly, an iambic pentameter line), then the same line repeated, then a third line with a terminal rhyme that completes the stanza:

The moon looks lonesome when it's shining through the trees;
The moon looks lonesome when it's shining through the trees.
And a man looks lonesome when his woman gets ready to leave.

The blues began, apparently, the way all music begins, as chant and as song. It's quite probable that in the earliest blues form the first line of a stanza was repeated, not twice, but three or more times, until the singer, who might be improvising (and who was possibly accompanying himself on some sort of stringed instrument), arrived at a good way of completing his thought and at an appropriate rhyme for his third line. The blues song thus evolved into a kind of poetry, and that point is worth dwelling over.

"I'm goin' down to the railroad," wails a typical blues verse, "and lay my head on the track."

"Yes," the singer declares, "I'm goin' down to the railroad, lay my head down on the track."

"When that train comes in," he concludes, "I'm gonna pull it right back."

That kind of wit, and its hint of self-criticism, are typical of the blues.

In the middle Thirties, when the men who wrote about jazz and other popular music began to discover the blues, they sometimes said that this musical form expressed (in the phrase of the times) "social protest." Certainly some of the blues do. They are about hard labor, poverty, a mean straw boss, and even racial segregation. But the blues are not ways of railing at conditions. They are art, and therefore they are ways of coming to terms with conditions aesthetically.

There are vivid blues about men dealing with nature. "The river has gone to rising, and spreading all over the land," one blues from the Twenties begins. But most blues are about men, dealing with other men, dealing with women, and sometimes dealing with themselves: "I just have to holler, because I'm just too mean to cry." Or there is this kind of personal insight:

I tossed and turned and cried the whole night long.
Yes, I tossed and turned and I cried the whole night long.
When I woke up this morning, I didn't know right from
wrong.

The words of the blues are sometimes just that
poetic. And an isolated and apparently simple line
can be moving:

Woke up this morning with the tears standing in my eyes.

More than likely, the singer just quoted had the
tears standing in his eyes because he had been badly
treated by his woman. The courtship of man and
woman is a main subject of the blues. Sometimes a
courtship includes love: "I was in love with you before I learned to say your name." But sometimes,
there doesn't seem to be any love involved:

Give your woman a dollar bill, and the next time, she'll
ask you for five.
Give your woman a dollar bill, and the next time, she'll
ask you for five.
Women don't give you nothin' back but a great long line
of jive.

Sometimes the poetry of traditional blues has a
wonderful air of mystery to it. "Oh, the sun's going to
shine in my back door some day" (yes, the *back*
door!), goes a line that can be heard in a dozen older
blues, and some new ones too.

In addition to the individual lines, and pictures of
life that they conjure up, blues talk about experience.
This is the way an old blues describes a youngster's
first sight of his first love:

It was early in the morning when I was on my way to
school;
Early one Monday morning, and I was on my way to
school.
That was the morning that I broke my mother's rule.

Another favorite stanza that turns up in various
forms in several blues shows a man trying to cheer
himself up, with ironic good humor, after his woman
has left him. It goes more or less this way:

No one on my mind. No cares, I'm keeping to myself.
No one on my mind. No cares, I'm keeping to myself.
You see, the girl that I love has found somebody else.

Then there is a good recent blues, written for Ray
Charles by Jesse Stone under his pen name, "Charles
Calhoun." It is called *Losing Hand.* "I gambled for
your love, baby, and held a losing hand." The singer
describes his love affair throughout as if it were a card
game which he lost by fate; he took his chance but he
was really doomed from the beginning.

There is one blues lyric I have saved because it is so
haunting. It was sung by a man named Robert Johnson and it is called *Hellhound on My Trail.* It is a
chant about spiritual torment, of a man pursued by a
demon. Here are some lines from it, with the singer's
repeating asides:

I got to keep moving, I got to keep moving . . .
Blues falling down like hail, blues falling down like
hail . . .
I can't keep no money, hellhound on my trail
(hellhound on my trail, hellhound on my trail . . .)

I can tell the wind is rising, leaves shakin' on the tree
  (shakin' on the tree),
I can tell the wind is rising, leaves shakin' on the tree . . .

During the Twenties some blues singers, particularly the great women singers of the time, were often
recorded with several instrumentalists. The players
not only "accompanied," but also improvised musical
comments on the meaning of the song behind and
between the singer's phrases. The balance among the
vocal performance, the poetry of the verses, and the
strength of the accompaniment became quite sophisticated, each contributing but none overpowering the
others. This special relationship among singer, song,
and accompaniment can be heard in the recordings of
one of the greatest of blues artists, Bessie Smith.

However, this brief discourse on blues poetry has
gotten us a bit ahead of ourselves. It was inevitable
that this vocal-poetic form should have been transferred to instruments. And so it was, and thus did the
evolution of music in all cultures repeat itself in the
United States. Blues singing, however, like most singing in the world outside the European concert hall
and opera house, was done with a great many "bent"
notes, glides and quavers of the voice, and other practices, to convey emotion. And as the blues idiom
began to be transferred to European instruments,
these "vocal" inflections and effects were retained by
the players. They discovered ways to play these
sounds on their instruments, and thus we hear jazz
horns laughing, growling, sobbing, and even using a

scale that employs notes not properly found in European music. As the instrumental music continued to
develop, a very unusual and interesting thing happened—instead of gradually being refined away, these
"vocal" effects were retained and even further developed. And they continued to be used by jazz musicians when they were playing in musical forms other
than the blues.

By the Twenties, it was common to hear purely
instrumental blues made entirely by the horns and
rhythm in a relatively sophisticated manner. In such
blues playing the musicians often made their melodies
without reference to a main theme, using the basic
outline and simple harmonies of the blues as their
only guide. Thus, on King Oliver's 1923 recording of
the fast and happy *Dippermouth Blues*, the leader
plays his celebrated plaintive solo of three blues
choruses that has no direct reference to the main
theme, but uses only the blues outline. And this "playing the blues," this improvising within the twelve-
measure blues outline, continued and developed over
the years. It was and is standard practice in jazz, and
almost any LP recording of jazz of whatever style or
school or period will probably contain one or two
twelve-bar blues pieces and sometimes more. Some will
use a standard blues theme to introduce the improvising, some a new blues theme (and every day provides
several new themes in this traditional form), and
some are simply ad lib from the beginning, with no
"main theme," only the improvised solos.

Now suppose I invent a new melody on an outline

borrowed from a standard popular song (say, *Dinah* or *Tea for Two* or *A Foggy Day*) and do not use the original melody at all. Could we not say that, in effect, I am playing the blues on an outline or a chord structure other than a blues chord structure? That is, that I am applying blues practice to another structure? Actually, one might say that during the late Twenties and Thirties, jazz musicians discovered that they could apply the principle of "playing the blues" —that is, of making up melodies with only a chord structure in mind—to structures borrowed from standard popular songs.

As I say, I don't think that when we listen to Charlie Parker's *Embraceable You* we should necessarily listen beneath Parker's improvised melody for Gershwin's outline. The outline is Parker's guide, not necessarily the listener's, and the main point is the melody that Parker is making, whatever his guide. The same might apply to a player using the blues outline for his guide. We should listen to the melody he is making, not to the outline.

But the blues form is basic to jazz and widely used in all schools and styles of jazz, as well as in other kinds of American music. Therefore it is probably a good idea to get thoroughly familiar with the blues idiom, perhaps even to the point where we do hear the underlying outline, the chord structure of the blues, and recognize immediately when jazz musicians are "playing the blues."

Obviously, some careful listening to blues performances is in order. A good place to begin is with any familiar vocal blues that uses the three-line stanza form we have given above: the opening line, the repeat, and the third line with the terminal rhyme. Listen, for example, to Count Basie's *Sent for You Yesterday*. The record has several instrumental choruses and two vocal choruses by Jimmy Rushing, all on a blues outline. Once we are thoroughly familiar with Rushing's vocal choruses, we will probably sense that the instrumental choruses fit the same outline. At this point it is very good ear training to sing the vocal choruses to the strictly instrumental chorus on the record. The next move would be to sing favorite blues vocal choruses to an entirely instrumental Basie blues from the same period, like *One O'Clock Jump*.

At the same time, we can learn a great deal by approaching the instrumental blues historically. We might begin with Sidney Bechet's *Texas Moaner* (Bechet was a superb blues player, particularly of slow blues), move on to Louis Armstrong's *Muggles*, then to Basie's *One O'Clock Jump*, then to the Modern Jazz Quartet's *Bluesology*.

It might be a good idea through all of this to keep singing those Jimmy Rushing verses, or some other favorite blues verses, with each of these pieces in succession, hearing how the same vocal line will fit with them, sensing how the cadences and chords fall and where the choruses stop and start. That is, it might be a good idea to do that if that's the way one enjoys approaching music. Further, it might be instructive even to count off the choruses mechanically for a while. The most common form of blues, the one we have been discussing, is the twelve-measure blues. Since most jazz is in four-four time, this means that if we count the beats, four at a time, we will have finished a blues chorus if we count to four twelve times. So, count off a chorus of Sidney Bechet's *Blue Horizon:* 1 2 3 4, 2 2 3 4, 3 2 3 4, 4 2 3 4, 5 2 3 4, 6 2 3 4 ... and so on, up through 12 2 3 4. I realize this sounds mechanical and, perhaps, even a little difficult. But with a little practice it isn't very difficult, and for some people the rewards in listening can be quite worth the trouble.

In any case, since the blues is an original American form, and since so much of our music is directly in that form, we should all probably know something about it. Indeed, it seems to me that if we are to have any acquaintance with our music at all, we should learn to recognize the American blues.

I should mention that we have dealt here with the twelve-bar blues only, and that the vocal versions that I have given of the twelve-bar blues are actually the simplest.

There are "refrain" blues also in the twelve-measure form; *Why Don't You Do Right?*, *Blue Suede Shoes*, and *Rock Around the Clock* are familiar examples of "refrain" blues. If we turned the first blues quoted earlier into a refrain form, we might get something like this:

The moon looks lonesome shining through the trees,
And a man looks lonesome when his woman packs to
leave.

You're mean to me, woman,
Meaner than I treat myself.
If you can't do better
I'll just get somebody else!

If you see me coming, raise your window high;
If you see me leaving, hang your head and cry.
You're mean to me, woman,
Meaner than I treat myself.
If you can't do better
I'll just get somebody else!

The commonest and most durable form, vocally and instrumentally, is the twelve-measure blues. It is brief, and under the severest technical scrutiny it hardly exists at all, yet, technically and emotionally, it has proved to be a flexible, adaptable, and enormously expressive poetic and musical vehicle.

A technical note: musically, the twelve-bar blues is thus a basic harmonic outline. In its standard form it usually appears this way: four bars on a I chord, two bars on a IV chord, two bars on I, two bars on V, plus a final two back to a I chord. Put into the common instrumental key of B flat, this would be, four measures on a B flat, two on an E flat, two on B flat, two on F, two on a B flat. A number of variations on this basic pattern, and a number of sometimes quite complex "substitute" patterns, are used. (These "substitute" blues-chord changes are not necessarily limited to "modern" jazz, by the way.)

When the "folk" blues first began to be written down and formalized (work in which W. C. Handy took an important part), the bent notes, the quavers, and the other vocal effects were approximated by putting certain notes of a major scale into minor— usually the third, sometimes the fifth, and usually the seventh notes of the scale. Actually, the blue notes are not minor notes in a major scale, but either by striking a minor note in a major context or by striking the major and the minor together, a pianist can approximate a quavering quarter tone, which is more or less what a blue note really is. A horn player can "lip" such a note, but a pianist cannot (although Thelonious Monk has a way of "bending" a piano note by a particular manipulation of his finger positions and keys and the foot pedals). Furthermore, it is not really accurate to say that the blue notes are the third, fifth, and seventh steps of the scale. In practice they may come anywhere, although we can say that instrumentally they tend to gravitate to the third, fifth, and seventh.

As we have said, we have dealt here only with the most common kinds of blues, the twelve-measure blues. There are also eight-bar blues, which more or less condense the twelve-measure form; the best-known example is probably *How Long Blues*. And there are sixteen-measure blues of several kinds. Some more or less spread out the twelve-measure form. Some adapt traditional sixteen-bar song forms on the order of, say, *Old MacDonald Had a Farm*; titles from *I'm a Ding Dong Daddy* through Sonny Rollins' *Doxy* fit this pattern.

RECORD NOTE

The Count Basie numbers cited here (*One O'Clock Jump, Sent For You Yesterday*) are included in "*The Best of Basie*," Decca DXB 170.

Robert Johnson can be heard on Columbia CL 1654.

A version of *Dippermouth Blues* by King Oliver is in Epic LN 16003.

Sidney Bechet's *Texas Moaner* is in his RCA Victor album, LPV 510, and his *Blue Horizon* is on Blue Note BLP 1201. Louis Armstrong's *Muggles* is in Columbia CL 853, "*Louis and Earl*." The Modern Jazz Quartet's *Bluesology* is in Atlantic 2-603.

Columbia has a series of albums by the great blues singer Bessie Smith. In addition to their sometimes sophisticated balance among singer, song, and accompaniment, these blues performances often involve interesting alliances of twelve- and sixteen-bar patterns in the same piece. Probably her most moving performance in the basic twelve-bar blues is *Lost Your Head Blues*, which may well have been ad libbed in the recording studio. Perhaps her best single performance is the more complex *Young Woman's Blues*, the words to which have been included in volumes of American poetry. Both are in the third volume of Columbia's "*The Bessie Smith Story*" (CL 857).

BOOK NOTE

Until there appears a book of blues poetry, there is a substitute in *The Book of the Blues*, edited by Kay

Shirley, with notes by Frank Driggs, published by Crown Publishers and Leeds Music. Lyrics are included, of course, but the transcriptions of the music (most of them taken from recordings) are sometimes accurate and sometimes formalized and "corrected."

Eight Recorded Solos

I Can't Give You Anything But Love
by Louis Armstrong   COLUMBIA CL 854

On the surface Louis Armstrong functions as a vaudevillian, but beneath the genial stage manner there is a rare and complex musical sensibility. Perhaps the most important aspect of his talent is his ability to make the most majestic musical statements while sometimes using the most ordinary material as his point of departure. Of course, part of the effect of Armstrong comes from the fact that he is a commanding trumpet player and that he makes his musical statements so well. But perhaps more important than the technique is the nature of those statements themselves. His paraphrase of the popular melody *I Can't Give You Anything But Love* is an excellent introduction to his playing.

His opening solo here is a half-chorus on the melody. And, if the melody were not already familiar, the ensemble drones it out in a fairly "square" and quite literal manner behind Armstrong as he varies it. Armstrong's paraphrase is relatively simple; it consists largely of delaying the written phrases of the song, altering a few notes, and slightly hurrying other phrases. In this opening half-chorus there is never any question of what piece he is playing, even to the most uninitiated ears. But at the same time there is no question of the original dramatic eloquence he finds in this theme.

A trombone enters, finishes the chorus, and Armstrong undertakes a vocal chorus. His vocal style, as has often been said, is very much like his trumpet style. But I confess that for me, it is often less expressively complex in its import—a half-burlesquing, almost ironic approach to the song between the more striking and penetrating trumpet episodes.

The closing trumpet solo here is in that secret combination of grandstanding and art which Armstrong, because he is so emotionally honest a musician, can bring off. His departures from the theme-as-written are much more dramatic and far-reaching than in his opening solo, but these departures, along with his display of sheer brass technique, always have a musical logic and reason-for-being.

The version of this piece we have cited was recorded in 1929. In the late Thirties, Armstrong remade the piece (Decca DL 8327). And in the mid-Fifties he did it once again (Decca DXB 783). Comparisons among the three are enlightening. In the

Thirties version, he begins with a vocal and ends with a trumpet chorus. The approach is less dramatic than in his earlier recording; his stance is cooler and more subdued. However, the trumpet chorus is an almost complete melodic departure from the original, an invention less dependent on the written melody than even his earlier final chorus. The mid-Fifties version, played with a smaller and much better group, follows the sequence of events on the earlier version —Armstrong on trumpet for a half-chorus, a trombone solo, the vocal, and a final trumpet solo. Armstrong is more introspective, but at the same time he rediscovers something of the broad sweep of his earlier work. It is this kind of playing which his "touch" alone makes so moving, and which some of his imitators therefore turn into mere musical posturing and emotional bathos.

Two more suggestions about this man's work: Armstrong's trumpet paraphrase of Harold Arlen's *I Gotta Right to Sing the Blues* (RCA Victor LPM 2322), a good popular song, is more complex than his opening chorus to *I Can't Give You Anything But Love*, in part because Arlen's piece is a more sophisticated example of songwriting. Therefore it might be a good next step in digging into Armstrong's work. His opening phrase, for example, is an almost gross simplification of Arlen's, but its effect by contrast is sweepingly dramatic.

From the same period in Armstrong's career, there is a magnificent example, which we have mentioned before, of how the trumpeter transforms an inferior song, *That's My Home* (also on RCA Victor LPM 2322), particularly in his soaring final chorus.

Body and Soul
by the Benny Goodman Trio
RCA VICTOR LPM 1226

We will confine ourselves to the opening chorus here, shared by Goodman's clarinet and Teddy Wilson's piano, and to Wilson's half-chorus which follows it. But first we might say something about the structure of *Body and Soul* and of popular songs in general.

Body and Soul is in "song form," in its most typical guise, a form borrowed from Europe. Song form, in this version, consists of a "main strain," an opening melody, which occurs three times in each chorus of the piece, and a secondary melody which we hear only once. First, the main strain is run through twice in succession, exactly or almost exactly. Then we hear that second melody (called the "middle" or "bridge" or "release" or "channel"). The bridge is the part we tend to forget, since we only hear it once per chorus. It often moves briefly into a different key, by the way. Then we go back to the main strain and hear it a final time again exactly or almost exactly. If we assign each of these two melodies a letter, song form comes out AABA. Also, each part, A and B, is in musical measure, eight bars, eight measures, long. Therefore, the total musical length of the typical popular song is thirty-two measures per chorus. (As we shall see later, this AABA version is not the only song form found in our popular music, but it is the most frequent.)

The Goodman Trio's performance of *Body and Soul* begins without introduction, as Goodman plays the main strain through twice, A plus A. He plays it fairly straight, although he inflects and stretches and slightly delays certain notes—he interprets them, "pronounces" them in his own way. His departures from the original are undoubtedly fewer than Armstrong's would be, and in a less tasteful player than Goodman such inflections might easily lead to melodramatics.

Wilson takes the B part, the bridge. He, too, sticks fairly closely to the theme, but he uses his gentle technique to embellish it. Then Goodman returns to complete the chorus with the third and final version of the A theme.

Next comes Teddy Wilson's striking half-chorus solo. It is a calm understatement, but an entirely original one. Wilson uses the outline of half the piece, the harmony to A plus A, as his guide. And he improvises a fresh melody, unrelated to the original, not only in its notes but also in its phrasing and general contour. Furthermore, Wilson is *using* the piano and its unique resources in a way that he could not if he were simply playing a song, a vocal line, on the keyboard. Wilson knew that he had to make a complete statement in a half-chorus, yet a statement that would not stop things dead—end the performance as a whole—but would allow for more music to come.

Wilson's solo is a melodic gem, and it is also beautifully organized along lines we will take up later. In any case, it is already obvious that there is more to an inventive jazz solo than stringing phrases together.

The record proceeds of course. Suffice it to say here that Goodman comes back at this point, plays more emotionally, and undertakes to leave the written theme more boldly. Wilson also returns, and his melodic imagination is still working for him.

The Sheik of Araby
by the Coleman Hawkins Octet

RCA VICTOR LPV 501

A typical tenor saxophone improvisation by Coleman Hawkins is not based on the theme melody. It is based to some extent on what jazz musicians usually call "running chords," or what classical musicians call arpeggios. This technique is worth dwelling over briefly, if only as a matter of general information. A chord is of course a collection of notes which are struck simultaneously—something one can do on a piano or other keyboard instrument with obvious facility. To play an arpeggio means to run through the notes in a chord in succession—in European music, usually bottom to top or sometimes top to bottom.

As an improviser, Hawkins "thinks" of a piece of music as a series of chords (as do most jazz improvisers in one way or another), and his general approach is to play through these chords as arpeggios, to open them up and thereby form his solos. In fact,

Hawkins' harmonic knowledge is more sophisticated than that, and he can interpolate "passing chords" between the written chords, and so forth, but our brief explanation is a good enough preliminary comment on his style.

Hawkins' two-chorus solo in *The Sheik* is the kind that may dazzle musicians as a rousing display of his techniques. To the layman, it also has its excitements, but these are more apt to lie in its pattern, its gradual building. Hawkins' playing gets relatively more complex, his emotion builds as he proceeds. Almost anyone senses this aspect of his work.

At the same time, Hawkins makes his rhythms in a fairly regular manner. He is apt to accent every other beat, *heavy*/light/*heavy*/light/*heavy*/light/*heavy*/light —a kind of DA-duta/DA-duta/DA-duta/DA-duta.

Obviously, in less sensitive hands, a business of making arpeggios with fairly regular rhythmic accents could become quite mechanical, and it is a tribute to Hawkins that his playing does not.

From a listener's point of view, Hawkins' single-chorus solo on *Dinah* (with a Lionel Hampton group, and included on the same LP as above, RCA Victor LPV 501) probably has a few more surprises. There, once Hawkins has set up the expectation of regular rhythmic accents, he varies them tantalizingly.

The two further examples of Hawkins which make good first presentations of his work are two of his celebrated slow ballads, *Body and Soul* (RCA Victor LPV 501), and *The Man I Love* (Contact CN-3).

Hawkins' two-chorus *Body and Soul,* done in

1939 was, surprisingly, a hit recording, as well as a highly influential one among musicians. Its virtues are many, but it is a classic example of a gradual building over two improvised choruses, technically and emotionally, from relatively simple melodic lines to more complex ones with shorter notes and using more technique, plus a brief restoration of simplicity in an out-of-tempo coda (an extended ending). It is also, by the way, an example of the effectiveness of Hawkins' style, for his listeners usually professed to find the recording quite melodious, yet at no point does Hawkins touch Johnny Green's familiar theme except perhaps for a note or two toward the beginning—and some of the arpeggios are showy indeed.

The Man I Love depends less on an obvious gradual building than *Body and Soul* and more on a brief, but highly effective, rhythmic variety, momentary whirlings away from the regular DA-duta/DA-duta/DA-duta/DA-duta.

Doggin' Around
by Count Basie DECCA DXB 170

As we have seen, a popular song is often structured in such a way that each chorus involves repeats. In the AABA form, the A melody appears three times, and its harmony appears three times as well. And even if we don't use the melody of the popular song, but use only its harmony, that harmony repeats in cycles within each chorus. In a sense, Coleman

Hawkins' style depends partly for its sense of form and order on the fact that the chords of a piece repeat in such cycles beneath his improvised melodies.

However, if we carefully listened once again to Teddy Wilson's solo on *Body and Soul* (and it is a solo that always repays listening), we would notice that Wilson seems to use certain personal melodic ideas that are related, that seem to echo each other. Or he seems to develop one bit of melody from the preceding bit, and so forth. This sort of musical and melodic logic may seem elusive at first, but a little listening brings it out, and for many people bringing it out makes future listening more enjoyable and rewarding.

One good beginning, by the way, is to take a popular song like *Just You, Just Me* and notice that the middle part, the B theme, is actually a development of the A theme. In jazz, a good introduction is a good Count Basie piano solo, and his solo toward the end of *Doggin' Around* is a Basie classic.

Basie's style is apparently simple. One hears a succession of brief, right-hand melodic figures, stated with delicacy yet with a marvelous and subtle swing. Indeed, one may get the impression that Basie is a man who works with an absolute minimum of material, that his vocabulary consists of a stockpile of a few phrases which he shuffles together in slightly different order from one solo to the next.

However, listen again to *Doggin' Around*: a little idea springs from the preceding one, develops it a bit, simplifies it or adds to it, or lengthens it, or shortens it, or merely accents it differently. One change suggests another change. Every now and then, a little phrase seems to be introduced for contrast. But the next phrase may tie the two preceding together into a third.

Probably one need not mention how monotonous such an approach to melodic order could become for a less imaginative player. But Basie's moment toward the end of *Doggin' Around* is the sort of solo to play over and over. To make a subjective confession about it, I've been hearing it for over twenty-five years, and, simple as it is, my next listening may tell me something new about it. Perhaps that is a good working definition of "art."

Jive at Five
tenor saxophone solo by Lester Young with the Count Basie Orchestra DECCA DXB 170

As we have noted, a Louis Armstrong solo may partly depend on glimpses of the original melody for one aspect of its organization.

And a Coleman Hawkins solo depends partly on the way Hawkins gradually builds it in musical complexity and in emotion, and also partly on the cyclical repetition of a bass line, of the underlying chords, a recurrence we may sense without actually hearing.

Lester Young's approach is almost opposite to that of both Armstrong and Hawkins. His typical solo, like Hawkins', is nonthematic, but the import of his playing is in contrast to Hawkins. His sound is lighter and airier, his rhythms more unexpected and varied, and his melodies clearer (and, in fact, less harmonically exact) for all their frequent surprise twists. He will seem, to almost any listener, I think, more directly melodic than Hawkins. His sense of order is also quite different.

He has the first solo on *Jive at Five,* a split chorus. The piece is a jazz original, but it uses the AABA song form. Young opens with a half-chorus, Harry Edison's trumpet takes the bridge, and Young returns for the final repeat of the A part.

Lester Young's sense of order here depends on linking phrases, somewhat in the manner of Basie. His first phrase is a precise little riff. His second begins in a slight contrast to that first phrase, but ends by echoing it. His third spins off logically from that second. And so forth. Even trumpeter Harry Edison starts his solo with the last idea that Young had used, and develops that into the melody. And Young comes back with a kind of musical "yes, but . . ." return to his original exposition and argument.

Some of Lester Young's solos do seem less organized than this one, and those of his imitators certainly are less well made. Sometimes Lester Young seems to depend on a bursting variety of ideas and surprises. But a little listening will often reveal that while he dances ad lib, Lester Young is often logical as well.

Embraceable You
by Charlie Parker
PARKER LP 407 OR ROOST LP 2210

Ornithology
by Charlie Parker
PARKER LP 407

Charlie Parker's alto saxophone chorus on *Embraceable You* does not use Gershwin's theme, and it is perhaps the supreme example of how a great player has organized a spontaneous melody around the appearance, reappearance, and transformation of a single melodic fragment, employing it in the subtlest manner.

We have mentioned this remarkable improvisation before, but it will be useful to look at it in more detail. After a piano introduction Parker opens with a little six-note phrase. He repeats it five times, "pronouncing" it slightly differently each time (and always in his own way, of course) and moving it around so that it fits Gershwin's harmonic structure, which Parker is of course using as his guide. On its fifth appearance, the little phrase forms the first notes in a long thrust of melody which after a break comes to rest with still another version of that original six-note phrase. From this point on, as he builds his chorus, Parker uses the phrase in various guises and permutations, interweaving it in his melodic fabric in sometimes delightfully unexpected ways. It may turn up with fewer notes or more notes or slightly different notes, but each use echoes its first appearance in some way—its first and all its other appearances as well.

Parker's use of this little recurrent musical motive helps him in giving form to his solo improvisation. At the same time, however, he gradually builds this chorus from simplicity to complexity and at the end to brief simplicity again, an upward and downward curve of melody, rather like Hawkins' pattern.

It happens, incidentally, that at the same recording date Parker did another "take" of *Embraceable You* which was issued briefly but which is now out of print. On this second take he played a completely different chorus melodically, and instead of building gradually he alternated simple and brief phrases with long and complex ones in a kind of back-and-forth contrasting pattern of tension and release, tension and release.

In his *Ornithology* solo (the piece, as we have noted, takes its harmonic structure from the popular song *How High the Moon*), Parker may seem to be depending on an altogether opposite effect from that on *Embraceable You*. *Ornithology* has great variety —it seems to burst with ideas, unexpected turns of phrase, striking rhythms. Perhaps it is Parker's sheer inventiveness that holds it all together. It is that partly. His rhythmic imagination is more complex than Hawkins', and even than Lester Young's; Parker's heavy accents not only fall on beats that would be "light" to Hawkins, but he is even more apt than Young to come down hard at various places between beats. At the same time, he never loses his way rhythmically or harmonically.

Still, the *Ornithology* solo has some nice patterns in

phrasing. Parker's opening technically covers about two bars of music. His second bit of melody however is one bar. His next bar is silent (and for all his dazzling technique Parker knew the value of musical rest). Then he plays another short phrase, then a long one, then three short ones—the last quite short (only two notes), then a quite long one, and a short one, and so on. Thus, without being in any way mechanical about it, Parker has built a kind of varied pattern in long and short phrases.*

(The Parker solo on the version of *Ornithology* issued on Baronet LP B105, by the way, is from the same recording session as this one, but has a quite different solo.)

We might mention that both of these pieces, *Embraceable You* and *Ornithology*, like *The Sheik of Araby* are in a different and less common version of song form than *Body and Soul*. This is a bridgeless version, consisting of sixteen measures of a main strain plus another sixteen that are a slight variant of the first. Again using letters for each section, we would

---

* A brief technical point: We said above that Coleman Hawkins tends to think of a piece of music as a series of chords, and that his solos are characterized by arpeggios in which he plays out the notes in the chords in succession. Parker also thinks of a piece as a succession of chords; thus in his celebrated *Ornithology* solo he uses E/—/Em/A7/ D/—/Dm/etc. But to Parker, as to Teddy Wilson (and to most jazzmen), each chord implies not only the notes in that chord but others as well. And Parker improvises by selecting notes proper to each successive chord and forming these into a continuous melody. Hawkins' style thus might be called vertical, Parker's horizontal.

describe this song form as "AA'."

As a note on our comments on Parker's *Embrace-able You*, we can recommend a solo by one of Parker's most brilliant "pupils," vibraharpist Milt Jackson, and the excellent developing melodic logic of his improvisation on *All the Things You Are* (Prestige 7421).

Lonely Woman
by Ornette Coleman ATLANTIC 1317

We have had examples of players who have depended somewhat for a sense of structure on the cyclical repetition of underlying harmonies, and examples of players who have depended on a more logical structure within their own melodies to give development to their improvising. Suppose we remove the cyclical bass line, the chord structure, and allow the player to make his melody, using it either in a very high-handed way or not at all. Let him depend on his own devices alone for his melodic ideas and his over-all design in his solo. This is the essence of the "free jazz," the "new thing" music of which Ornette Coleman is an artistic leader. Thus, although Coleman is original, he should not be too "difficult."

Lonely Woman, since it introduces a recent style in jazz as well as Coleman himself, is worth describing in some detail, I think. It begins with bass and drums juxtaposed, each playing a different rhythm. Then, the horns—Coleman's alto saxophone and Don Cherry's trumpet—enter, quite unexpectedly, and in a different rhythm still, with the passionate, dirge-like theme that is *Lonely Woman*. It is obvious that in this style, and even playing this way in an ensemble, each of the two horns is allowed interpretive leeway, the kind of lee-way that only a single player would be allowed in a theme-statement in previous styles. That is, each man plays the melody, inflecting it in his own way, al-though both play it at the same time (Coleman going it alone briefly at only one point). Furthermore, the "intonation," the "pitch," of the two horns seems odd or oblique, or simply "wrong." Coleman's words on this are interesting; he says, "You can play sharp in tune and flat in tune." What this oblique pitch amounts to is an extension of the idea of the "blue notes" of earlier jazz. Not only occasional notes, but whole phrases and episodes can be played "blue," deliberately.

Lonely Woman borrows song form (roughly), and Coleman plays the bridge portion as a solo. Here we become more acquainted with something that was evident earlier and will be even more evident later: that Coleman enunciates his melodies so that his horn almost speaks, more so even than earlier jazzmen and bluesmen. Yet at the same time he is an instrumental-ist, making a music appropriate to the alto saxophone; he is not merely imitating a singer or speaker on a horn.

Coleman's main improvisation is one chorus long, and on this occasion he does have the outline of the piece in mind. Indeed, Cherry comes in to accompany him under what is clearly the bridge portion. But Coleman does not use the chords to the piece in any regular manner. He does organize his playing melodically, however, in much the same manner that we have heard Teddy Wilson and Count Basie and Lester Young and Charlie Parker doing: an idea appears, is extended, developed, turned around one way and another. It may yield another idea, or another may be simply introduced for contrast. At the same time, Coleman obviously sustains and probes the mood of his piece of which his title is a perfect description.

We may also notice here that the drummer's interplay with the soloist is more varied than on previous records—that bass and drums don't so much "accompany" soloist as they do on earlier records. To be sure, in all jazz the juxtaposition of the rhythms implied in the soloist's melody and those of the rhythm section is a part of the music's effectiveness.

Lonely Woman is a good introduction to Coleman's playing. So is another Coleman performance, a rhythmically engaging piece called *Ramblin'* (Atlantic 1327). So also is his solo in the first section of Gunther Schuller's work based on *Criss Cross, Variants on a Theme by Thelonious Monk* (Atlantic 1365), where Coleman deliberately goes slightly counter to the group rhythmically, and seems hardly at all interested in Monk's chords or structure, but does improvise around Monk's theme.

At this point, one may want to plunge into Ornette Coleman's *Congeniality,* which has a remarkable, intricate, extended solo using several sequential ideas. These phrases occur, are gradually transformed, are dropped, perhaps to reoccur in still other permutations.

What Does a
Composer Do?

A "line" to a jazz musician is a melody that opens a performance, usually by a small group. It is what classical players would call a theme statement. In a quintet or a sextet in any jazz style except dixieland, this "line" will often be played in unison by the horns, accompanied by the rhythm section. The line, more often than not, sets up a series of harmonies, a chord structure, on which the players proceed to improvise. It may also set up a melody, of course, if any of the players want to use that melody in their choruses. And it should in some sense set up a mood.

Let's briefly look at two examples of original jazz "lines" in two classic quintet performances.

Now's the Time and *Billie's Bounce* by the Charlie Parker Quintet

SAVOY 12079

The two lines come from the same recording date and are both from the same composer, Charlie Parker; they are both ways of introducing the blues and are both in the key of F. They were both probably presented without a written score to the members of the group by Parker at the recording session; they were memorized and played.

In every other respect, however, the lines are different. *Now's the Time* is based on a traditional-sounding jazz "riff," typical of the "swing period" jazz of the Thirties, perhaps—a little rhythmic phrase which is repeated over and over, but moved around to fit the harmonic contours of the twelve-bar blues, and thereby changed slightly at some points—simple and highly effective. As we hear it, however, we do notice that Parker has given it a couple of original touches, particularly in its ending. The basic riff involved in *Now's the Time* may sound quite familiar because it is the same riff that became a "rhythm and blues" hit in the middle Forties as *The Hucklebuck*.

A typical performance of *Now's the Time* begins (perhaps after a brief introduction, usually by piano) with the horns—in the recording discussed here trumpet and alto saxophone—playing the theme in unison, once or twice. They play it once or twice more at the end of the performance. In between, each of the horns, and perhaps also the piano, will improvise some blues choruses.

Billie's Bounce is performed in much the same way, but it is obviously a more complex and intriguing melody. It sounds almost like a good jazz solo. At a casual hearing, that may mean that it sounds like a succession of different phrases, in contrast to *Now's the Time* which seems, at first, a repetition of the same phrase. But there is more to it than that; for all its variety, *Billie's Bounce* is well organized. After we have heard it a few times, we may notice that the second phrase and the last phrase are the same, or almost the same. Perhaps it is a kind of musical tapestry, then, with contrasts and likenesses. That second phrase almost interrupts the first and deliberately contrasts with it. The third phrase is a logical development of the second. And so forth.

As we have said apropos of well-patterned solos, we may sense such musical logic without specifically hearing it. We can begin to hear it with a little listening. But if we decide that we take no particular pleasure in listening with such exactness to music, we can still recognize the general differences between the two blues lines *Now's the Time* and *Billie's Bounce*, and perhaps agree that each is effective in its way.

Incidentally, the LP listed above on which these two are available is further enlightening in that it offers several "takes" of several pieces, all recorded by the same group during the same recording date. We can hear the pieces develop and change as the players try them out and learn them and arrive at a satisfactory version.

Parker's contribution to these two blues performances, then, is as the composer of two themes and as an improvising soloist. He has not really "orchestrated" the themes for the group, nor has he designed the performance in any but the most casual way.

On the other hand, a jazz "composer" may sometimes not compose, but use the themes of another, giving them some kind of written orchestration—which in jazz is usually called an "arrangement." Our chapter title is therefore something of a misnomer in that jazz composers are often composer-arranger-orchestrators, or sometimes simply arranger-orchestrators.

Let's take two examples of jazz versions of standard popular melodies as treated by jazz arrangers.

Sometimes I'm Happy
by the Benny Goodman Orchestra
melody by Vincent Youmans/arrangement
by Fletcher Henderson

RCA VICTOR LPM 1239

Smoke Gets in Your Eyes
by Thelonious Monk Quintet
melody by Jerome Kern/arrangement by
Thelonious Monk   PRESTIGE 7363

Fletcher Henderson's orchestra was one of the first to arrive at a style for big-band jazz, a way of realizing jazz for a larger dance orchestra after the triumphs of the early New Orleans styles. The Henderson style was evolved chiefly by an arranger named Don Redman, but Henderson subsequently undertook composing and arranging himself. Between 1932 and 1934, his orchestra not only realized a big-band jazz style, but evolved some of the arrangements that Benny Goodman played a few years later when Henderson wrote for Goodman's orchestra.

Basically, Redman and Henderson started with a dance-band style and made it into a jazz style.

Henderson's *Sometimes I'm Happy* was quite a celebrated arrangement. (Goodman incidentally has recorded it several times and, aside from the original version listed above, he has done basically the same scoring for Columbia, Decca, and Capitol records.) Briefly, Henderson offers an introduction and three and a half choruses on Youmans' melody. In the course of it, he allows a trumpeter, a tenor saxophonist, and a clarinetist to improvise.

Henderson's introduction is a kind of summary-in-front; it uses Youmans' ending plus some of the effects that Henderson will introduce later. In the first chorus, muted brass plays the Youmans melody fairly straight, but between its phrases, the saxophones swing a little effect which, we soon realize, comes from worship, from a congregation's response ("Yes, indeed!" or "Yes, my Lord!") to the preacher's sermon.

The first half of the second chorus is a trumpet solo. In this version it is played by Bunny Berigan and is an interesting original melody. The half-chorus saxophone solo which follows is less good but, in using the theme more than Berigan does, it is perhaps an appropriate contrast. Henderson's third chorus is a written variation on the theme; the first half of it is written for the saxophones and the second half for the brass. This kind of written, section variation is typical of Redman and Henderson, and this particular chorus has been praised for its naturalness—for sounding rather like a jazz improvisation.

The climactic portion of the score comes next as Goodman's clarinet exchanges improvised phrases with somewhat bolder writing for the brass. Then comes Henderson's ending, a brief, effective understatement.

The arrangement is unpretentious and has an agreeable variety. The improvisation in the second chorus produces a certain excitement with which the calmer, written variations that follow contrast. And the final clarinet and brass effects are a nice (although obvious) climax.

In one sense, the score is simply Youmans' *Sometimes I'm Happy* "in the jazz style"—with the virtue that Henderson was one of the people who discovered what that jazz style could be.

Monk's quintet arrangement is both more straightforward and more complex and sophisticated. Monk does not so much play Kern's *Smoke Gets in Your Eyes* in the jazz style; he digs more deeply, he recomposes—he transmutes song into a composition for instruments. By the most apparently simple means, Monk has taken Kern's pretty tune and made it a thing of beauty.

There are two choruses here, in a sort of miniature "concerto" style. Monk's brittle piano sound offers an obviously semi-improvised part, while the warmer trumpet and tenor saxophone play "written" (more likely, memorized) parts. Actually, Monk has scored very little for the horns—eight bars, and they play them several times—but the effect is anything but repetitive, especially as they are juxtaposed with the varied piano part.

Monk has not given himself the theme, assigning the horns only in accompaniment. He has split the melody up somewhat so that the horns get some of its notes, although his piano gets most of them. Also, Monk has revised the melody in simple but masterful ways so that its original notes plus his new ones create a rich new theme. The result is not simply an old melody hung with embellishments and decorations. (By the way, he has slightly but tellingly revised Kern's harmony, too.)

If there is anything to add to this general description in the way of details, it would be to draw attention to the "middle," the "bridge," of the first chorus, where the drummer, Art Blakey, responding to Monk's improvised ideas, briefly doubles up the rhythm. This effect is echoed in the beginning of the second chorus. That section starts as a straight piano solo, and is further from the original melody than any other part of the performance. Finally, there are Monk's witty and musically effective *tremolos* (literally, moments when he makes the notes tremble) in the second bridge.

Now let's take some examples of jazz scores on original jazz material. And to make comparisons that are even more interesting, we will limit ourselves to several examples of instrumental blues.

Dead Man Blues
by Jelly Roll Morton RCA VICTOR LPM 1649

The record starts with some talk, a brief and supposedly comic verbal exchange. Actually, the trombone introduction that follows sets the tone of the performance. The player used the beginning of the Chopin funeral march, played with a breathiness that is almost comically ironic but is basically serious.

The first chorus is offered in what we recognize as the New Orleans or "dixieland" style. Three instruments, trumpet, clarinet, and trombone, play three melodies simultaneously. The style may remind us of the classical style called counterpoint, as in Bach's music. But it isn't quite the same, because in counterpoint all of the simultaneous melodies are equal. In New Orleans jazz, the trumpet (or occasionally two trumpets) carries the main theme, the clarinet's more lacy and intricate melody is secondary, and the trombone's simpler part (which lies somewhere between the horns and the rhythm section that accompanies them) comes third. (The "classical" term for this New Orleans style would be *heterophonic*.) The New Orleans ensemble playing on *Dead Man Blues* is very delicate, excitingly intricate, beautifully balanced— far more sensitively performed than most dixieland playing. And it has a marvelous light momentum which is quite unlike that of the heavy dixieland ensembles, with strident horns and plodding rhythms beneath them, which we are used to in this style.

Following this fine opening ensemble, there is a one-chorus clarinet solo by Omer Simeon, a variation on the previous theme and a touching, nostalgic melody.

Next comes a trumpet solo of two choruses. It is the sort of jazz solo which in its general contours is worked out ahead of time, and which in execution allows for only a few changes. The player here is George Mitchell, and Mitchell's solo is based on a second theme for *Dead Man Blues*. *Dead Man* is built in several sections or parts or themes, like many rag-time pieces and dixieland standards, and like W. C. Handy's blues (*St. Louis Blues*, *Memphis Blues*, *Beale Street Blues*). Mitchell's solo is also conceived as a two-chorus whole, not as a simple succession of one chorus plus another chorus. (As noted elsewhere, in the version of *Dead Man* currently available, we hear a warm-up solo from Mitchell in which he makes an unfortunate mistake. Nevertheless, one can gain an idea of how good an arrangement this is and how appealing a player Mitchell was.)

So far, then, we have had a complex, heterophonic ensemble, and two solos of different lengths. Next we hear the third theme of *Dead Man*, performed in harmony by three clarinets, a saucy, dancing melody, a nice contrast to the two preceding sections. The three clarinets balance Mitchell's solo by playing this melody through twice, two choruses. But the second time through, the trombone moaningly performs a secondary theme beneath them.

This two-part performance leads to the final chorus, which is a three-part variation on a theme. That is, it returns to the complex style of the opening chorus, with the trumpet on top, the clarinet weaving in and around it, and the trombone singing more simply beneath them. This final three-way ensemble has the same delicacy as the opening one, but has more drive and a little more swing, as befits a climax.

Thus, Morton's *Dead Man Blues*, a three-minute gem. Balanced at the beginning and end with choruses in a similar style, and based on solo and ensemble themes and variations in between. It moves from one chorus to the next with good design, yet at the same time Morton obviously also saw it whole. If one were to add one or two choruses more to *Dead Man*, he would probably destroy it. Subtract a chorus, and one surely would. Transpose any of its parts, trade around or reshuffle its choruses, and one would ruin Morton's fine miniature design.

At the same time, the performance holds in an almost perfect balance what is written and what can be changed in performance, what is up to the individual and what is assigned to the group.

One O'Clock Jump
by the Count Basie Orchestra

DECCA DXB 170

Main Stem
by the Duke Ellington Orchestra

RCA VICTOR LPM 1364

Basie's *One O'Clock Jump* is probably the most effective big-band, medium-tempo blues of its kind. It helped "make" the Basie orchestra in the late Thirties, and as borrowed by others (with and without acknowledgment) it helped make popular a few other swing bands as well. It is the sort of arrangement that was gradually worked up in performance by the members of the Basie band, and only written down later (if at all). It is a quite casual, string-of-solos performance.

It begins with two choruses by the leader's piano in his typically spare, apparently simple style. At the end, Basie's last phrase changes the key. Quite possibly the reason for the key change was that, at this tempo and in this optimistic mood, Basie liked to play the blues in one key and the horn players, in another. But the modulation does add variety and sets off the leader's episode.

There follow one-chorus solos by saxophonist and brassmen (trombone and trumpet), back and forth. The first is Herschel Evans on tenor saxophone, then George Hunt on trombone, then Lester Young on tenor saxophone, then Buck Clayton on trumpet. Each player gets a different background figure or riff, and the sax players are accompanied by brass riffs, the brass players by saxophone riffs. So far, everything is appropriate and obvious, even the fact that a trumpet makes a good climax, so a trumpeter is given a climactic solo.

As one might expect, the most brilliant player does the most interesting thing: Lester Young's background is a rather fancy little figure played by the brass. Young begins his solo by playing a light parody of that figure going on behind him. Then he develops his parodic opening phrase into a one-chorus melody.

After Clayton's trumpet high point, piano punctuates a chorus of simple, "walking" notes by Walter Page's bass. Then follow three ensemble choruses. These choruses are the thing that makes the *One O'Clock Jump* the *One O'Clock Jump*. Otherwise, it might be any big-band blues of the period. In all three of these final choruses, the trombones and trumpets play the same figure—an upward slide on the trombones followed by three darting notes from the trumpets. The saxophone figures, juxtaposed on the brass, do change from chorus to chorus. The general effect is quite exciting while, at the same time, being obviously controlled.

One O'Clock Jump has little over-all design and wasn't intended to have much. In performance, it might be extended almost indefinitely—by giving each soloist more than one or two choruses, by introducing other solists, trying out new background figures, and so on.

As the sort of arrangement gradually evolved by the members of an orchestra as they play the blues night after night, *One O'Clock Jump* had no single "arranger." However, some jazz scores are worked out in ways almost opposite to Count Basie's *One O'Clock Jump*. That is, they are put together by a composer-arranger, working on his own, and are then presented to an orchestra to perform. The arranger offers written parts and places for solos, in many of which he allows the solo players to ad lib.

But the best jazz arrangements so far have usually been collaborative efforts between a composer, who may also be an orchestra leader and player, and the members of his orchestra, with their individual talents as players and improvisers. These arrangements have also taken good advantage of the various sounds and combinations of sounds possible in the jazz orchestra. And they have had an over-all sense of pattern, design, and development. Perhaps the best way to elaborate these points is to pick an example and listen to it in some detail. Almost inevitably that example will need to come from the Duke Ellington orchestra, for Ellington has always worked in close association with his players, individually and collectively, with perceptive knowledge of their talents and how those talents might be brought out, and with a keen sense of overall design in a given piece of music and a given performance of that music. Frequently, in the resultant music, it is difficult to tell exactly what Ellington has contributed to a piece and what his players have contributed, separately and together. But it is not difficult to conclude, after experience with his music, that Duke Ellington himself provides a focal point for everyone's talents, including his own. "He plays piano," his collaborator Billy Strayhorn once said, "but his real instrument is the orchestra."

Ellington's *Main Stem*, although slightly faster than *One O'Clock Jump*, may seem to be just the same sort of casual, big-band, string-of-solos performance. Of course there is the obvious difference that the performance opens with an ensemble theme and closes with a reprise of that theme, whereas *One O'Clock Jump* uses ensembles only at the end.

But let's hear *Main Stem* in more detail. The opening theme is not a simple riff, but a more sprightly and imaginative projection of the kind of riffing we heard in the Basie arrangement, a more interesting melody. And there is the way this melody is scored and presented. Typically, Ellington doesn't use his orchestra section by section as Henderson and Basie do, with the saxes playing one thing, the trumpets playing another, and sometimes the trombones playing a third thing. In the opening to *Main Stem*, we hear what sounds like *some* trumpets (with *some* kinds of mutes in them), *some* trombones (with *some* kinds of mutes in *them*), with perhaps *some* saxes, somehow joining for unexpected and interesting rhythms, sounds, and orchestral colors.

Next, the Ellington soloists take over, chorus by

chorus. They are, in order: Rex Stewart on cornet*
(with the growl-like effects of what is called a
"plunger" mute); Johnny Hodges on alto saxophone;
Stewart again, on open horn; Ray Nance on open
trumpet; Barney Bigard on clarinet; Joe Nanton on
"growl," plunger-muted trombone; Ben Webster on
tenor saxophone; Lawrence Brown on trombone.
Then, the theme is reprised.

However, there is more to *Main Stem* than a string
of solos. And there is more to the backgrounds they
are given than simple riffs. Stewart's opening solo is a
somewhat argumentative conversation between himself and some saxophone figures that are based on a
simplification of a portion of the main theme. Hodges,
the more intricate melodist, gets no background.
When Stewart returns for his typically querulous,
open-horn solo, he gets as a background a sketch of
the opening theme. Stewart himself uses that theme in
his solo, but not in a way that repeats the background.
Ray Nance uses the theme not at all, and in his background the main theme is almost completely restored.
Bigard makes some slight use of the theme, and his
background is theme-like but played by the brass. In
Nanton's background the saxes predominate.

Between Nanton and Ben Webster there is a written interlude by the ensemble. Something very interesting is happening, for Webster's solo is not a twelve-
measure blues chorus. It is longer, a sixteen-measure

---

* The cornet is closely related to the trumpet and some
listeners (including some musicians) profess to hear little
difference between the sounds of the two. Others heartily
disagree.

blues chorus. Ellington has introduced a new section into this piece, in effect a secondary theme. Webster's chorus is lyric and there are new figures behind him. Lawrence Brown's chorus which follows is more robust, and it is again built on the secondary, sixteen-measure theme. Here Ellington puts brass figures behind Brown's brass instrument. Finally, when we return to the main theme, the ending is extended; there is a four-measure "tag," and thus the final ensemble chorus summarizes not only the twelve-measure choruses but also the longer choruses given to Webster and Brown.

Ellington's *Main Stem* is obviously much more of a "whole" than the Basie blues. Backgrounds tie it together, for one thing. One would not want to reshuffle these choruses, and one could not uproot a chorus from *Main Stem* and drop it into another blues. And the piece seems satisfying for its approximate three-minute length; one would not want it much longer or much shorter, and one would not want the solos doubled up.

Main Stem is not the most carefully designed of Ellington's scores, to be sure, but it is a good introduction to Ellington's sense of form and a good contrast to the Basie piece.

Let's take one other example from Ellington, only a part of a performance this time, an introduction and three choruses only that introduce a vocal blues.

· · ·

I Don't Know What Kind of Blues I Got
by the Duke Ellington Orchestra

RCA VICTOR LPM 1364

Ellington's piano introduces the piece and he uses his keyboard effects to set a mood and to suggest musical colors. In the first chorus, Barney Bigard's clarinet plays a blues theme in the lower register, while Lawrence Brown's trombone plays a counter-melody behind him. In the second chorus, the brass performs a variation on Bigard's opening theme, while Ben Webster's tenor saxophone improvises a counter-melody behind them. In the third chorus Bigard comes back to paraphrase his theme again, this time in the upper register, high on the clarinet. And Lawrence Brown returns behind Bigard to do a variation on the theme he had used in the opening chorus.

This beautiful three-chorus opening gives an idea of what may and what may not be improvised in Ellington, and how much improvising is sometimes involved. The brass in the second chorus is of course playing a preset part. And the soloists embellish spontaneously, but they obviously need to stick fairly close to an assigned melody if the patterns of echo and contrast in these three choruses are to work out well. Webster, on the other hand, has an original theme and is probably departing furthest from any preassigned melody. But at the very least each player is allowed to *interpret* his part fairly freely, even if he must play certain of its notes. And the three choruses are an example of how good Ellington's orchestrations can be even on an admittedly minor piece.

An even more carefully wrought Ellington twelve-bar blues is *Ko-Ko* (RCA Victor LPM 1715). An equally well-wrought score, and a very subtle use of the eight-bar blues, can be heard in *Blue Serge* (RCA Victor LPM 1364). Ellington's masterpiece outside the blues form is probably his *Concerto for Cootie* (for trumpeter Charles "Cootie" Williams) (RCA Victor 1715). There is also a marvelously designed small-group Ellington blues called *Blue Light* (Columbia CL 2126). But Ellington, as a master composer-arranger, has high achievements from all periods of his career.

Misterioso
by the Thelonious Monk Quartet
BLUE NOTE 1510

In Monk's small ensembles, "orchestration" is sometimes as improvisational as some of the solos in certain big-band performances. Yet at his best Monk has a rare sense of over-all, compositional form, and is a superb composer of jazz themes.

Misterioso begins, without an introduction, directly on the pianist's blues melody. Like many of his themes, this one sounds both traditional and original; Monk has found exceptional music by reassessing an old "walking" blues bass figure. The opening is stated by Monk and vibraharpist Milt Jackson, with the bass and drums phrasing with them on the accents of the piece rather than playing "time" behind them. After the theme chorus, Jackson, always a brilliant blues player, begins to improvise. Behind him Monk gives a stark and intriguing accompaniment, built around one note. Monk is obviously not accompanying Jackson in the usual way, simply by playing the chords of the blues behind him, as most pianists would. Monk plays something more interesting, and certainly more assertive, than blues chords. And his accompaniment seems to be holding the piece together in an orderly way, making it, at this point, not merely Jackson playing the blues (however brilliantly) but Jackson playing Monk's blues, *Misterioso*. Monk's notes under Jackson seem somehow related to his main theme, yet not exactly.

That theme, technically speaking, is based on the sixth notes of the appropriate scales. Monk's accompaniment to Jackson's chorus is based on the next implied note, the seventh. In Monk's solo, a sense of order continues; and he builds his improvisation around an ascending figure which echoes the upward, "walking" movement in his main theme.

When that theme is reprised at the end of the performance, it is carried by Jackson, the bass and drums accenting with him. This time Monk does not play with Jackson but *against* him, partly spreading out his previous accompaniment to Jackson, juxtaposing it against the theme. Thus Monk provides a one-chorus summary of the whole performance. It is a brilliant intuitive stroke, and *Misterioso* uses a kind of loose, extemporaneous "arrangement" that is the equal in its way to an orchestrator's careful scoring.

It's interesting to compare this version of *Misterioso* to a less successful "take" recorded at the same session by the same group (Blue Note 1509). Then, one might move on to other classic Monk on the same label, *Criss Cross,* and to the fascinating *Evidence* where Monk's intriguing theme is hinted at in the introduction and the accompaniment, to emerge at the very end—and then only in a semi-improvised and approximate form.

In almost any of these performances, by the way, one can note the fine rhythmic and melodic expressiveness that Monk gives to musical space, openness, rest and fleeting silence, both in solo and accompaniment.

Bluesology
by the Modern Jazz Quartet
ATLANTIC 2-603

The instrumentation here is the same as on Monk's *Misterioso,* and Milt Jackson is present in both groups. The approach to form is similar, but more casual here and with some differences. *Bluesology* itself is a relatively simple blues "line" by Milt Jackson, and the "arrangement" is a matter of the group's performance.

The recording opens with a brief introduction which hints at Jackson's melody. Then the theme is stated twice, Jackson mostly carrying it. First time through, the drums and bass play a kind of stop rhythm; the second time they play continuously. Jackson takes the first solo, and he improvises for six choruses, building to a relatively complex fourth chorus and then to a rather *bravura* sixth. Behind him on piano, Lewis, like Monk, does not accompany only with chords. Lewis' accompaniment almost reaches way back to the Basie blues, for he uses basically simple, repetitive riffs. But he does not leave them so simple; he uses several successive riffs in a short space and develops the whole into a more complex running melody. This melody interplays with Jackson in a way that echoes the heterophony, the simultaneous improvising, of New Orleans ensembles. Yet Lewis doesn't really interfere, and is always alert to the intricacies of Jackson's improvised lines.

The complexity of this interplay reaches a peak as Jackson ends his portion of the piece. Lewis' solo is shorter (four choruses) and simpler—his style is simpler and Jackson doesn't accompany him. The calmer episode is appropriate. (Incidentally, Lewis has some favorite ideas that have evolved as he has played this piece over the years and they generally show up in his solos on *Bluesology*, although they take a different turn from one performance to the next.)

After Lewis' solo we hear one chorus of more or less arranged riffing interplay between Lewis and Jackson, simple and almost static. Jackson reintroduces the more mobile theme and it is played once more against a semi-stoptime—as if to retard the performance and bring it to an end.

Bluesology is not the most intricately nor best designed of the Modern Jazz Quartet's performances. But it is done very well and it does introduce one to their sense of form. It also shows how the group's penchant for design has evolved in performances which undoubtedly began with the basic, string-of-solos approach. Finally, *Bluesology* makes a good comparison to the several other blues in the album listed above, *Pyramid, The Cylinder,* and *Bags' Groove.*

The group's masterpiece of composition, design, and performance is John Lewis' *Django.* The Quartet has recorded it three times, has played it hundreds of times, and it seems a constant source of renewed inspiration. Anyone who wants to dig more deeply into the Quartet's work and into modern jazz in general, could do well to hear and re-hear the different recordings of *Django* and absorb them. They are on Prestige 7425, Atlantic 1325, and Atlantic 2-603.

Django is a funeral processional, a cortege, for the Belgian-Gypsy guitarist-turned-jazzman, Django Rinehart, and its opening theme manages to convey that complex excellently. As a performance of *Django* unfolds, we see that something else was in Lewis' mind—the tradition of consolation and rejoicing at death that was a part of New Orleans culture and of early jazz, a tradition also echoed in Morton's *Dead Man Blues.* A simple but lively bass figure, as old as jazz and perhaps older, appears during the first improvised choruses as a counter-motif, suggesting this ambivalence. As it reappears, it draws the improvisers from their pensive introspection. Lewis himself often uses another dancing blues fragment to accompany it, particularly in later versions of the piece. Gradually there is a kind of emotional resolution between these opposing moods of sadness and joy by the time the main theme re-enters.

The delicate movement and range of feeling of *Django* is an achievement in itself. Its melodies and counter-motifs are excellent; and the act of holding this complex together and formally sustaining a work of this length is rare in jazz. The piece also has the basic necessary quality of a jazz composition of being able to inspire good improvised solos.

One final suggestion: as a comparison, one can hear three members of the MJQ, with Horace Silver on piano in place of John Lewis, in an informal recital on which Jackson plays beautifully on Prestige 7655.

Last Trip Up the River:

A MUSICAL GUIDE TO JAZZ HISTORY

Although there were scattered written commentaries from earlier dates, current jazz criticism in the United States has its roots in work done during the late Thirties. That work was largely biographical; at its worst, it was sentimental or anecdotal enthusiasm about those colorful old characters who played jazz. Theories about the way the music had evolved were largely imported from France and were probably accurate enough for their time. They held that jazz came up the river from New Orleans to Chicago, there remaining largely pristine, but then went to New York and became something called "big-band jazz."

A more elaborate version expanded on those geographical hints. It had jazz going up the river from New Orleans, stopping off for a while at St. Louis, and resting at Chicago. Then everybody piled into Model T Fords and Stutz-Bearcats and took off for

New York, where jazz became uptown New York Style and downtown New York Style. Following this, it somehow jumped out to the Middle West to become Kansas City style. Then back to New York to become what was at first called re-bop.

Another version used some style names instead of city names to subdivide essentially the same theory. It held that there was original Negro New Orleans jazz, derivative white dixieland jazz, and then there was swing, largely a big-band style. There had also been, one used to admit with a vague gesture toward a distant past, something called ragtime. This approach has been expanded to include the more recent catch-names, be-bop, cool jazz, West Coast jazz, hard bop, funky, free-form jazz or "the new thing," and so on, *ad* (it may turn out) *exhaustium*.

Ah, and already we have several obvious flaws, for St. Louis was a center of ragtime before the turn of the century, so what did New Orleans jazz encounter there, coming up the river in the late Teens and early Twenties? And surely both Chicago style and downtown New York style intended to be sophisticated refinements of basic dixieland. And surely the players of Kansas City style were actually working out some of the rhythmic and melodic implications of Louis Armstrong's style; they had things in hand by about 1932. By 1936 and the Basie orchestra they had them down so well that the musicians could relax and play around with them. And surely most jazz since the mid-Forties has been strongly indebted to Charlie Parker, whether it is called bop, cool, or funky. These things being so, surely our theories of jazz history, musically speaking, are a useless tangle.

If we look at jazz history without reference to maps, but with only the concrete musical evidence of recordings, the first firm artistic fact we encounter is that from the mid-Twenties through the late Thirties Louis Armstrong's genius as an intuitive improviser affected the work of every jazz musician. Certainly as a soloist, Armstrong inevitably had his imitators. But more important, he had his legitimate followers who worked out some of the implications of his style for themselves without doing imitations.

That Louis Armstrong was a powerful and compelling player should go without saying. He also had a more sophisticated sense of harmony and melody than any who had gone before him, and he gave the music a new stylistic language. Further, he had a rhythmic sense that was not only surer than what had gone before him but different, and, as André Hodeir pointed out in *Jazz: Its Evolution and Essence* (Grove Press), his rhythmic message was the essence of his contribution to jazz.

It is no coincidence that the word *swing* came into use among musicians while the music was under Armstrong's tutelage, for it is their word to describe his idea of jazz rhythm. He could play a phrase that had been around long before his time, but he would inflect it, accent it, pronounce it in such a way that it had a very different impetus and momentum, and this basic rhythmic impetus opened up the music to twenty years of development in melody and harmony as well.

In short, his influence was profound, and from 1923 to 1943 most jazz, big band or small, is significantly "Louis Armstrong Style."

If we pick the next most important artistic fact in jazz after Armstrong's arrival and 1932 peak, it would surely be the maturity of Duke Ellington as a composer-arranger and bandleader. Ellington's function was not personal like Armstrong's, but rather that of a catalytic leader of a group of musicians, and his greatest contribution was not in discovering a new language—although his orchestral language was and still is exceptional and highly personal and involved the transmutation of a vast storehouse of devices into the jazz idiom. Ellington's contribution is that he discovered form for jazz, form that went beyond a succession of individual improvisers.

Equally obvious is the fact that the next great event in jazz music after Ellington's 1938–42 maturity was a period in which the artistic leadership fell largely to alto saxophonist Charlie Parker. Again, as with Armstrong, the music had an individual, intuitive improviser reinterpreting the jazz language and influencing the music pervasively for nearly twenty years. And again, the basic contribution was rhythmic. The thing that characterizes Parker's playing and that so many people found so new in his work (new and, for some, disturbing) was its rhythm, not so much the innovations in harmony and melody that were associated with this rhythmic character. Parker's accents fell on strong beats, weak beats, and in various places between beats. Technically, one might say, with a certain gross but perhaps necessary simplification, that Louis Armstrong's idea of jazz rhythm is based on a quarter note and Parker's on an eighth note.

Actually, almost every harmonic device of modern jazz can probably be found somewhere or other, say, in the "experimental" music of the downtown New York schools of the Twenties, which centered around Red Nichols, Miff Mole, and various followers of Bix Beiderbecke. But on a Nichols record deliberate harmonic sophistications are apt to sound stilted and even naive, whereas in Dizzy Gillespie and Parker and Monk they sound perfectly natural and forceful. I suspect this is so because Nichols' associates were stiff and jerky rhythmically.

The musics of Armstrong, Ellington, and Parker are the dominant musical facts of jazz between the late Twenties and the early Fifties. And in them there is a kind of pattern, from Armstrong's innovations to Ellington's synthesis to Parker's innovations. One might expect then that by the late Fifties modern jazz would begin to find *its* synthesis in the work of a composer-arranger. And that is precisely what happened.

Upon Parker's death, musicians began to rediscover Thelonious Monk, and in his small groups Monk had rediscovered form. It was different from Ellington's form, freer perhaps, certainly more improvisational, but a good Monk performance is also all of a piece, and (to simplify a bit) his continuity often depends on the leader's orchestral concept of his piano keyboard and his almost uncanny ability to fragment his composed themes as a part of his accompaniment and as a part of the melodic logic of his solos.

I do not think that Monk was alone in discovering appropriate form in modern jazz, for performances by the Modern Jazz Quartet have it, too. Monk also had a superb "pupil" for a while in tenor saxophonist Sonny Rollins.

If our scheme so far does describe some kind of pattern for jazz music, one might have expected by the late Fifties that the next major event following Monk's rediscovery of form would be further innovation guided by a single player. Again, that is precisely what happened in the arrival of alto saxophonist Ornette Coleman. Inevitably, Coleman's work remains "controversial" in the trade and fan press, but not among most young jazz musicians. In him we again see innovation that is basically rhythmic— he has a fresh and unexpected way of accenting and phrasing his melodies as he builds them, and he has allowed (one hopes for good and all, although he was not the first) for spontaneous collective changes of tempo within a single performance.

Thus, our scheme of jazz history involves a gradual evolution in rhythm, and a kind of pendulum swing from innovation to form to innovation to form. And it seems to me this scheme is given further confirmation even in pre-Armstrong music, where a paucity of recordings or reliable scores makes the historian's problem much more difficult. There was, for example, an important composer-arranger who discovered orchestral form in a pre-Armstrong style: Jelly Roll Morton. Morton did use a few devices from later styles (an increasing use of solo improvising was one), and his major orchestral works were recorded late, after Armstrong's career had begun. But clearly he represents an earlier era, and from his first piano solos, made in 1923, through the orchestral pieces made in 1928, Morton's music presents form and synthesis of what jazz had achieved up to the time that Armstrong entered and began to redirect its course.

Rhythmically, I think we can go back even further than that. Judging from the scores that survive, the earliest American minstrel tunes seem to have been based on one heavy beat per bar, that is to say a rhythm based on a whole note. Think of the vestiges of this in a familiar piece like "RUfus Rastus JOHNson Brown." Later minstrel songs had a cakewalk rhythm of two heavy beats per bar—think of how the cakewalk was danced on alternate high kicks. If we try to put our minstrel song into such a later rhythm, it might go "RUfus RAStus JOHNson BROWN."

Ragtime, while it thrived (roughly from 1895 to 1910), seemed a bold and daring stroke. It no longer seems so today, but the thing that was so "raggy" about it then was that it added syncopations to the cakewalk rhythm. If we think of the late cakewalk as "ONE two THREE four/ONE two THREE four," then ragtime might be "ONE and a TWO and a THREE and FOUR." Louis Armstrong might play our earlier piece something like this: "RU-FUS RAS-TUS JOH-HON-son Brown."

(We can also, by the way, extend our ideas into later jazz-influenced popular music: for two quick examples, George Gershwin's rhythmic idiom is pre-Armstrong; Harold Arlen's is post-Armstrong.)

This capacity for rhythmic growth is the thing that keeps jazz alive and able to maintain its identity. Without it, jazz might long ago have entered the genteel limbo of "light" music, with the *The Syncopated Clock*, never to return. And there is nothing whatever in its outer environment that would insure such original rhythmic growth; on the contrary, everything in its environment would seem to insure a borrowed harmonic expansion once jazz had begun to absorb European practice, as it did longer ago than anyone knows. But harmonic sophistication would not necessarily make good music.

I realize that my theory of jazz history involves some simplifications; players like Bix Beiderbecke, Lester Young, and Charlie Mingus, for examples, in addition to their intrinsic merit have often predicted developments several years before they appeared fully. But I don't think such a scheme precludes precursors any more than it precludes individuality within a period or style, once one of the great figures has established that style. To take a random sampling, Teddy Wilson, Roy Eldridge, Coleman Hawkins, and Vic Dickenson do not merely copy Louis Armstrong. They learned major lessons from him, they very possibly learned minor lessons from others, and they contribute something of their own. Similarly, Milt Jackson, Miles Davis, and John Lewis do not "copy"

Charlie Parker. And art cannot exist only by its geniuses, nor should a listener confine himself only to them.

Like any artistic theory, the one offered here has its limitations. Art behaves much like human life and resists rigid categories. But this seems to me a sound view of what has happened in jazz—sounder, at least, than one that would involve piling up more geography or fashioning more stylistic catch-phrases. It is, at any rate, one way of bringing some order to the history of a music that has seemed to change constantly and rapidly in its sixty or seventy years. It is also, I think, a way of showing that changes in jazz are not the result of caprice or fashion, but are sure signs of artistic life.

BOOK NOTES

The best jazz history is still Marshall Stearns's *Story of Jazz* (Mentor). The second best is probably *Hear Me Talkin' to Ya*, edited by Nat Shapiro and Nat Hentoff in 1955 from the comments of musicians themselves.

Leonard Feather's *New Encyclopedia of Jazz* (Horizon) is a standard reference work.

A more specialized history is *They All Played Ragtime* by Rudi Blesh and Harriet Janis (Grove). The book does stretch its definition of ragtime to include what is probably more usefully called "jazz heavily influenced by ragtime."

Gunther Schuller's *Early Jazz* (Oxford) is an excellent critical study.

Other examples of good technical criticism include André Hodeir's *Jazz: Its Evolution and Essence* (Grove), which, however, sees jazz as beginning artistically with Armstrong, and, by the same author, *Toward Jazz* (Grove). There is also Leroy Ostransky's *The Anatomy of Jazz* (Seattle).

Impressionist jazz criticism can be found in Whitney Balliett's volumes, *The Sound of Surprise* (Dutton) and *Dinosaurs in the Morning* (Lippincott).

There are many volumes of jazz biography, particularly of early figures, and inevitably their quality varies. However, Sidney Bechet's *Treat It Gentle* (Hill and Wang) is one of the most eloquent autobiographies ever written by an American artist.

My own book *The Jazz Tradition,* which is a study of seventeen major jazzmen, and which develops some of the same ideas of jazz history found in this book, is forthcoming from Oxford. I have edited the anthologies *The Art of Jazz* (Oxford) and *Jazz Panorama* (Collier), and written paperbacks on *King Oliver* (Perpetua) and *Jelly Roll Morton* (Perpetua).

A series of biographical studies of jazzmen, taken decade by decade (more or less), with myself as general editor is being published by The Macmillan Company. *Jazz Masters of the Fifties* by Joe Goldberg, *Jazz Masters of the Twenties* by Richard Hadlock, *Jazz Masters of the Forties* by Ira Gitler, and *Jazz Masters of New Orleans* by myself have appeared.

A Basic Library of Jazz

On the basis of our preceding outline of the main events in jazz history, we could arrive at a basic, beginner's collection of jazz on LP more or less as follows:

Jelly Roll Morton, *"King of New Orleans Jazz"*
RCA VICTOR LPM 1619

Louis Armstrong, *"A Rare Batch of Satch"*
RCA VICTOR LPM 2322

Duke Ellington, *"At His Very Best"*
RCA VICTOR LPM 1715

Charlie Parker, *"Bird Symbols"*
PARKER RECORD 407

Thelonious Monk, *With Milt Jackson*
BLUE NOTE 1509

Ornette Coleman, *"The Shape of Jazz to Come"*
ATLANTIC 1317

The list needs a few comments. In putting it together, we are attempting to capture each artist at his best—or his best on records so far—but of course an artist's importance is more than just a few examples of his best work. Also, we are (I hope) dealing with currently available long-playing records. All of which is perhaps a way of saying that a beginning collection is only a beginning, and perhaps a bit arbitrary at that.

Inevitably, these LP collections are not entirely ideal. For instance, we must issue the warning that, although there is a great deal of excellent music in a Jelly Roll Morton LP, including Morton masterpieces like *Kansas City Stomps* and *Black Bottom Stomp*, another Morton masterpiece, *Dead Man Blues*, has been dealt with rather badly; as we have seen, on this LP transfer somebody spliced in a trumpet solo from another "take" of the piece. We can still get an insight into *Dead Man Blues*, but there *is* still a wrong note by the trumpeter (something that may bother the listener, even if he doesn't know it's a wrong note).

Likewise, our Louis Armstrong collection has such sublime Armstrong as *I Gotta Right to Sing the Blues*, *Basin St. Blues*, and *That's My Home*, but it does not include his great version of *Sweethearts on Parade* because that belongs to another company. Nor does it have *I've Got the World on a String*, which is included in another RCA Victor Armstrong LP. And a great deal of important Armstrong can be found in the Epic and Columbia catalogs.

For the Ellington LP, we can say that the music included comes from his great period, and includes the *Concerto* for trumpeter Charles "Cootie" Wil-

liams and *Ko-Ko*. But it does not have a third Ellington masterpiece from the time, *Blue Serge*, which is
on another of Victor's Ellington collections.

The Charlie Parker collection is probably the best
single Parker anthology. It has *Ornithology* and *Embraceable You*, for example. But it will probably be
found only in very well-stocked record shops or in
stores specializing in jazz. However, there are some
substitutes for it, as we shall see below.

The Monk selection is actually currently issued
under Milt Jackson's name, and in addition to the
work with Monk includes Jackson with a very early
version of the Modern Jazz Quartet. However, there
is classic Monk in *Criss Cross*, *Eronel*, *Four In One*,
Evidence, but on another Blue Note Monk LP there is
a better version of *Misterioso* than this one.

Finally, in Ornette Coleman, we pick only what
seems the best introduction to his work so far.

So much for a basic, basic set. Now let's try a more
comprehensive library of jazz. Again, the collection will
be somewhat arbitrary in its details. It depends in part
on what is currently in print, although, in resisting a
temptation to dwell on the gaps in the jazz LP catalog,
I have pretended that some rather hard-to-get LPs are
not quite so hard-to-get. The list also inevitably depends
on my own idea as of this writing of what a basic library
should contain.

I've broken the collection down into different categories. Of course they should not be taken as absolute
or self-contained; they are merely guides which may be
helpful.

I. Backgrounds and sources in brief

An Anthology FOLKWAYS 2801
Robert Johnson COLUMBIA CL 1654

The Folkways anthology includes work songs and
"folk" dances and blues, some quite elementary, some
more sophisticated. There is even a dramatized sermon
with comments from the congregation. Particularly
moving is the unaccompanied, incantive chant to the
sun, a kind of *ur*-blues, called *Ol' Hannah*. The Robert
Johnson set is a collection by one of the most powerful
Mississippi blues singers, as we have said earlier, a man
who was an exceptional folk poet as well, as his verses
on *Hellhound on My Trail* demonstrate.

II. Ragtime

Joseph Lamb FOLKWAYS 3562
Hank Jones ABC PARAMOUNT 496

We have not dealt with ragtime directly in this
book. Let it be said that at its best it is not old-timey,
ricky-tik piano novelties. It is a relatively formal music,
originally designed for the piano. Each ragtime piece
will have three or four different sections, like a polka
or a march. Improvisation and variation were not
prominent in classic ragtime, although they were undoubtedly used in performances of it around the turn
of the century. Obviously, many early jazz pieces, dixieland favorites particularly, which have several sections
or themes, owe their structures to ragtime. Joseph
Lamb was one of the best rag composers; he was recorded as an old man, shortly before his death. Hank

Jones, one of the most accomplished journeymen jazz pianists who ever lived (he is a staff musician at CBS, by the way), plays rags today with a heartening authenticity and care. His LP is unfortunately delivered for half its length on a "prepared" piano, deliberately made to jangle. But the other half is not. One selection included is called *Jazz Mag Rag*. It is in no sense an authentic ragtime piece, being made up mostly of "swing period" phrases, but it serves as an instructive contrast to the authentic rags which are present.

Several other collections of good rags, most of them played by composers, have been transcribed from old piano rolls. They were originally issued on the Riverside label. Piano rolls sound somewhat mechanical, to be sure. The records are now out of print, but Milestone promises a similar series for the near future.

III. The New Orleans ensemble

King Oliver   EPIC LN 16003
Jelly Roll Morton   RCA VICTOR LPM 1649

The approaches of these two men to the simultaneous improvising of the New Orleans style are as different as they are alike. Morton's Red Hot Pepper music is polished and compositional; that of Oliver's Creole Jazz Band more casual. There is another Oliver collection which you may be able to turn up, on Riverside 12-122; some of the same music shows up on Orpheum 105. A revised and expanded version of the above-listed Oliver LP may be issued by Epic. Milestone's Oliver anthology (MLP 2006) has three titles by Oliver's Creole Jazz Band, and for two of them, interesting alternate takes, recorded at the same session, are included. And on Mainstream 6020 there is a quite charming piano and vocal recital by Morton.

IV. Soloists and singers from the Twenties

Louis Armstrong	COLUMBIA CL 851, 852, 854
Armstrong/Earl Hines	COLUMBIA CL 853
Bix Beiderbecke	COLUMBIA CL 844-5
Bessie Smith	COLUMBIA CL 855-858
Sidney Bechet	RCA VICTOR 510; BLUE NOTE 1201

The above can of course be supplemented in various ways. For example, Decca has an Armstrong album and a Jimmy Noone/Earl Hines album from the period with much interesting music.

V. The Thirties—big bands

An Anthology	FOLKWAYS 2808
Fletcher Henderson	DECCA DL 9227, DL 9228
Duke Ellington	RCA VICTOR LPM 1364, 1715
Count Basie	EPIC SN 6031

The Decca albums survey Henderson's career from 1924 to 1934, and are, I think, the best introduction to his work. A more comprehensive Henderson survey can be found in Columbia's anthology C4L 11. Among the Ellington albums from Decca, RCA Victor and Columbia, a good portion of the recording career of this remarkable musician may soon be either in print, about to be in print, or only recently deleted. The Basie anthology on Epic is available as LP singles as LN 3107 and LN 3168.

There are a number of 1930s and early 1940s big-band anthologies in the current catalog, by Earl Hines, Jimmy Lunceford, *et al.*

VI. The Thirties—soloists and singers

Louis Armstrong	RCA VICTOR LPM 2322
Red Allen	RCA VICTOR LPV 556
Roy Eldridge	MAINSTREAM 6037
Charlie Christian	COLUMBIA 652
	ARCHIVE OF FOLK MUSIC 6037
Coleman Hawkins	CONTACT CM-3;
	RCA VICTOR LPV 501
Art Tatum	20TH CENTURY-FOX
	TFM 3162-3
Benny Goodman Trio and Quartet with Teddy Wilson and Lionel Hampton	RCA VICTOR LPM 1226
Billie Holiday	COLUMBIA CL 627, C3L 21
Lester Young	COMMODORE 30014
Ella Fitzgerald	DECCA 4451
Ben Webster	VERVE 8274
Joe Turner	ATLANTIC 1234
Django Rinehart	CAPITOL TBO 10226

Of the categories so far, this one is probably the most arbitrary and difficult, both because of the nature and limitations of the current LP catalog and the nature of the category itself. Does the listener gain enough of an introduction to Red Allen or Coleman Hawkins from the Henderson entries above, or to Lester Young from the Basie recordings, not to need these further listings, or to find his own way to these if he is sufficiently interested? Do the Basie records introduce trombonist Dickie Wells, or should one add Prestige 7593, which has some celebrated Wells performances? Similarly, if the Basie sidemen get additional listings, why not the Ellington men? And still again, if Dickie Wells is listed, should Jack Teagarden also be? Etc.

Such being admitted, a few additional comments are called for. A possible substitute for the Armstrong set is Epic 22019, which repeats the two takes of *Stardust* heard on Columbia CL 854 and has a remarkable "second take" of *Between the Devil and the Deep Blue Sea*. The Eldridge album contains a couple of his best solos, but is actually listed under Coleman Hawkins' name. More good Eldridge is on the Mainstream trumpet album (6017). Selections from the Tatum albums have been issued on a cut-price label called Movietone. Emarcy 26011 has superb Hawkins and very good Teddy Wilson and Roy Eldridge on *I'm in the Mood for Love*—and such a listing of exceptional individual performances might go on indefinitely.

The second Charlie Christian album above actually comes from about 1941, and its music is somewhat transitional; it is one of the few recordings we have of informal musicians' jam-session performances. It and several albums listed are currently issued in an electronic stereo version which sometimes involves a distracting echo. (Turning off the stereo button will restore some of the original sound quality.) Incidentally, Christian's classic *Profoundly Blue* is on Blue Note 6505.

Further comments: There is very good Eldridge

available in Columbia's otherwise highly uneven anthology "*The Sound of Chicago*" (C3L 32), and on some selections in Columbia's Gene Krupa anthology (C2L 29). There should be a good collection of boogie-woogie blues piano of this period, but there isn't at the moment. And there should be a good, selective Fats Waller album; meanwhile there is RCA Victor LPV 516. Incidentally, the tenor saxophone soloist on *Early Session Hop* on the Hawkins Victor LP is not Hawkins, but Ben Webster. The material in the Lester Young set is also available on Mainstream 6012, but the label put the wonderful '*Way Down Yonder in New Orleans* on Mainstream 6002. Two more substitutes: for Art Tatum, Capitol T 216; for Billie Holiday, Mainstream 6000.

VII. Modern jazz—the innovaters

Charlie Parker	PARKER PLP 407;
	ROOST 2210;
	SAVOY 12000
Dizzy Gillespie	SAVOY 12020
Bud Powell	BLUE NOTE 1503
Sarah Vaughan	COLUMBIA CL 745
Lee Konitz/Lennie Tristano	PRESTIGE 7250

Parker presents problems in the current catalog. If the above cannot be found, the Verve series "*The Charlie Parker Story*" (8000–8002) has a few curiosities but also, for examples, some excellent quartet and quintet selections, a remarkable *Lady Be Good*, and a *Just Friends* and a *What Is This Thing Called Love* with string accompaniments on which Parker himself plays with a kind of divine vengeance.

Substitute Gillespie from the mid-1940s is a bit harder to come by, but half of Roost 2234 has an exhilarating 1947 Parker-Gillespie concert, and Fantasy 6003, a Parker-Gillespie concert of a few years later, with Bud Powell.

The Sarah Vaughan item is fairly arbitrary, as the recording career of this exceptional singer has been quite uneven. For her singing, the album "*Great Songs from Hit Shows*" (Mercury MG P-2-100) can be recommended, as can '*Tain't No Use* from Roulette 52060.

VIII. Modern jazz in maturity

Miles Davis	CAPITOL T 1974
Thelonious Monk	BLUE NOTE 1509, 1510, 1511
Modern Jazz Quartet	ATLANTIC 2-603
Horace Silver	BLUE NOTE 4017
Sonny Rollins	PRESTIGE 7326
Charles Mingus	IMPULSE A 54;
	COLUMBIA CL 1440

Once again, the limits of our category are fairly arbitrary.

There is a remarkable pair of Miles Davis "all-star" LPs, with the likes of J. J. Johnson, Milt Jackson, and Thelonious Monk, on Prestige 7608 and 7650, which might be added. There is the previously mentioned Monk solo recital on Riverside 12-235. Etc.

IX. The "New Thing"

Miles Davis	COLUMBIA CL 1355
Cecil Taylor	CONTEMPORARY 3562
Ornette Coleman	ATLANTIC 1317

ON THE SCENE

Monk at the Five Spot

The Five Spot Cafe in New York City sits at the corner of Cooper Square and St. Mark's Place. The address may sound a bit elegant unless one knows that St. Mark's Place is an extension of Eighth Street into the east side and that Cooper Square is the name given a couple of blocks along Third Avenue at the point where Third Avenue ceases to be called the Bowery. All of which means that the Five Spot Cafe is at the upper reaches of New York's now dwindling skid-row area.

It was once a pretty sordid stretch of sidewalk, this Bowery, but since the city removed the Third Avenue elevated train tracks and let the sunshine in a few years ago, the street has been given something of a face-lift, or at least a wash-up, and the number of alcoholics who stagger along, panhandle in, or recline on its sidewalks has declined constantly.

This current paucity of winos along the Bowery is only one indication of fundamental changes taking place in the general area of the east side below Fourteenth Street. There are, for example, about six prospering off-Broadway theaters there. And some of the old pawn shops and secondhand clothing stores have disappeared, to be replaced by collectors' book shops, paperback-book stores, and even a music store.

Right across the street from the Five Spot, an old greasy-spoon lunch room has been transformed into one of those chi-chi hamburger palaces, the kind where the counter is made of unfinished wood and the menu reads "beefburgers, seventy cents."

The area was once the upper end of New York's lower east side. But now it is being called East Village. And that nominal aspect of its transformation is coming about because a little more than ten years ago, the artists and writers and painters moved there from across town to escape the spiraling rents and the increasingly middle-brow atmosphere of Greenwich Village on the west side. The Five Spot owes its existence as a jazz club to these transplanted artists and the cultural interests they brought with them.

The current Five Spot Cafe is a fairly large room as New York jazz clubs go. One enters it under a neat sidewalk canopy which reaches from the front door to the gutter. He walks through a short vestibule, with its hatcheck booth to the right, and into a square, dimly lit room. The walls are painted a warm red, and the effect of contemporary decor is spoiled only by a couple of square columns in the center of the room that are encased in mirrors and look rather like surplus props from a 1936 Ruby Keeler musical.

A bar takes up almost the length of one wall on the right as one enters. To the left, at right angles to the bar, is a slightly raised platform, the club's bandstand. The wall behind the bandstand contains three archways leading to a kind of patio area where patrons are seated behind the musicians on crowded evenings.

9:30 P.M. The bar is full, although the relief group, the Roland Hanna Trio, is not due to start playing until 10 and Thelonious Monk's quartet not expected till 11. The bar looks familiar; it was moved from the original Five Spot, once a few blocks down the Bowery but now demolished for another of those grim, hazardous institutions known as modern housing.

According to the New York Fire Department's notice posted on a back wall, the club's occupancy is limited to 223. There are about 35 people now at the tables and more arriving. It is mostly a young crowd, the kind one would expect during a holiday weekend. The red walls are covered with posters and flyers for artists' showings and gallery openings and for jazz concerts dating back a year or so—just like the walls of the old Five Spot.

Across the room, a lone man sits at a corner table. A waiter, dressed in a neat, red jacket that almost matches the paint on the walls, says politely, "Sorry, sir, this is a table for four." The waiter looks like a college student on a part-time job, and he is.

A couple come in and are escorted to a table near the bandstand. She is wearing a mink, and he doesn't look old enough to have bought it for her.

In the patio area, there is a jukebox. To judge from its listed contents the clientele's taste runs to the Marvellets, Brook Benton, Nina Simone, and comedienne Moms Mabley. It isn't playing, however, but there is a piano LP being quietly piped through the house public-address system. The recorded pianist is heaping up currently hip block chords at a great rate.

It isn't very much like the old Five Spot. It is cleaner, neater, bigger, yet younger, more prosperous, and business-like but still very comfortable and easy as clubs go.

Behind the bar, Iggy Termini, a stocky, blond man of medium height, and co-proprietor with his brother Joe, is polishing glasses when he isn't filling them or checking some small account books he keeps back there. He and the bar itself are the familiar sights in a relatively unfamiliar atmosphere.

The original Five Spot was a neighborhood bar and had been in the Termini family for more than twenty-five years. It was not particularly a Bowery bar, for there are many such that cater almost exclusively to the thick tastes and thin pockets of the skid-row clientele. When the Termini sons, Joe and Iggy, came out of the Army, the father Termini gradually turned the place over to them. They in turn found themselves getting as customers more and more of the Village expatriates who had moved into the neighborhood. These included sculptor David Smart and painter Herman Cherry, both of whom hounded the management to put in some live entertainment—specifically, some live jazz. The Terminis finally capitulated.

The honor of being among the first musicians to play jazz in the Five Spot belongs to the David Amram–George Barrow group, to Cecil Taylor's quartet with Steve Lacy, to Randy Weston, and to Charlie Mingus. By that time, the future had clearly been decided, and this small east-side bar was a going New York jazz club.

It was rather a relaxed scene in those early days. There was no cover and no minimum, the beer was relatively inexpensive, and the listeners were attentive. In a sense there was too much listening; in order to handle the increasing crowds, Joe and Iggy had to take on some help and made the mistake of hiring a few younger jazz fans and hippies to tend the customers at the tables. As a result, something like the following scene was played with minor variations several times a night:

Customer: "Waiter, could I have another. . . ."

Waiter: "Shush, man! Don't you dig—Jackie is soloing? Wait a minute!"

It soon became house policy to interview a prospective employe carefully, and if he admitted the slightest interest in jazz, he probably wouldn't get the job.

The Terminis soon went after the then-legendary Monk for the Five Spot. They finally got him, and it was Monk's extended stays at the club that had as much as anything else to do with his rediscovery by musicians and critics as a major jazzman. The most celebrated of the several Monk Five Spot gigs was the first, in the summer of 1957, with Monk, tenor saxophonist John Coltrane, bassist Wilbur Ware, and drummer Shadow Wilson, a group and an occasion important enough to have become fabled within six months of its existence. And it was at this point that Joe Termini would acknowledge, in one of his relatively guarded moments, "Well, we're in show business now."

And after the triumphs with Monk? Well, the second most celebrated booking was surely the first New York appearance of saxophonist Ornette Coleman (who was also something of a fixture for a while), and there was a return engagement for pianist Cecil Taylor too.

Meanwhile, the Terminis had temporarily branched out with a second and larger club, the Jazz Gallery, a promising but ill-fated enterprise a few blocks up and across town.

Then, Charlie Mingus was back to close the original Five Spot before the wrecking crews moved in to demolish it.

Iggy and Joe acquired a corner cafeteria and tobacco shop a few blocks up the street, redesigned it, and applied for a license to operate a cabaret. They didn't get it at first, and for a while it was touch and go at the new Five Spot with legally allowable pianists, without drummers, and with some weekend sessions. They took in Hsio Wen Shih, son of a Chinese diplomat, former publisher of the *The Jazz Review*, writer on jazz, and architect by profession, as a part of the organization. Finally there came the license and an official opening with the current Thelonious Monk Quartet, an engagement which continued for seven months.

9:55. A male voice, young, drifts up from somewhere in the crowd that is drinking, chatting, and waiting for the music to start: ". . . swimming in the nude and that sort of thing, but they've clamped down on it." Roland Hanna, looking like a kindly but officious banker who is about to explain an overdraft to a befuddled dowager, enters the clubroom through the kitchen, crosses the floor to the area behind the bandstand (this patio area is the section that used to be the cigar store), and chats with his bass player, Ernie Farrow.

Behind the bar, Iggy says softly to an old customer, "This is a quiet place. I mean there're no problems." (He probably has in mind the Bowery drunks who used to wander into the old place and try for a handout before Joe could grab them and usher them out, thrusting them firmly among the crowd of fans that usually filled the sidewalk outside the club.)

A few feet down the bar, a young man who has been nursing a beer for about an hour says to his companion, "How about that rent strike in Harlem?"

10:05. Hanna moves out of the patio area, through an archway, and onto the bandstand. He sits down on the piano bench and warms up by running through the middle octaves of the keyboard. Farrow is in place. Drummer Albert Heath also looks ready. They begin, and Hanna's banker's demeanor continues through the thick chords of his opening chorus of *On Green Dolphin Street*. The crowd continues to buzz and chat. But then Hanna is interpolating a phrase from *Solar* and waggling his head, and the banker is a forgotten *persona*.

There is applause as the pianist segues into a bass solo, and it is followed by a sudden burst of irrelevant laughter from someone enjoying a private joke at the bar. A young man in a heavy, black turtle-neck sweater and olive-drab corduroys crosses the room, earnestly searching for the men's room door, snapping his fingers as he goes.

Hanna's right hand travels up the keyboard, and the number is over. Scattered applause.

Through the front windows of the patio, a city bus visibly grinds down the side street. At the canopy, a lone panhandler approaches a couple of arriving jazz fans.

The place is filling up, and the late arrivals are not so young as the earlier crowd.

10:20. Heath, in a long drum solo, has the eyes and ears of the crowd. At the end of the bar, a middle-aged woman looks on admiringly, and as if she knew exactly what was happening. She has a copy of *The New Yorker* and a half-empty martini glass on the bar in front of her. To her right, her escort looks non-committal.

10:40. Hanna, into a fast blues, laughs about the tempo during Farrow's long solo. At the front door a waiter takes down the rope for a couple in their late thirties and for four youngsters on a double date. The older couple ends up at the bar, and the foursome gets a table.

10:50. Frankie Dunlop and Butch Warren have arrived, but so far no Monk and no Charlie Rouse. Hanna finishes his set and announces into the mike that he is turning over the bandstand to "Mister high priest, Thelonious Monk." Shades of 1947 press agentry! A waiter confides to a customer at a back table that Hanna tongue-tangled it into "the high beast of pre-bop" a few nights back.

Various beards, bulky sweaters, and Brooks Brothers suits begin shuffling around the room, table-hopping, men's-rooming, and telephoning, as silence follows Hanna's departure from the stand.

Nobody turns up the lights between sets, and the red walls smolder on the right and left, to the front and rear.

"Did you ever see Monk's drummer?" asks a fellow at the bar, loudly for some reason.

A woman at a back table giggles constantly.

"Yes, Germany and Japan were *allies* during the war—you mean you didn't *know* that?" says he to her at a table by one of the mirrored columns.

"Ya, but ze Americans zey. . . ." says she, a young, blond girl looking earnestly at her escort.

11:20. "Look out!" someone shouts to a waiter near the center of the room. Behind him the dark figure of Monk is rushing down an aisle between the tables, singular of purpose and unmistakable in his tweed hat and heavy tan jacket. He is quickly through the kitchen door at the back end of the club, headed for the dressing room beyond.

11:27. Monk comes through the kitchen doors and moves toward the stand, a little more slowly this time but no less purposefully. He is hardly in front of the piano before he is playing *Don't Blame Me* solo. A burst of hard applause covers his opening notes, but almost immediately the room is silent. He plays with unrelenting and uncompromising emotion, and there is simply nothing to do but listen. Then a sudden, hard succession of clusters of tones in the bass. What did he *do?* Ah, anyway Monk is still growing. The second chorus begins with wild, sardonic trills, played partly with the inside fingers of the right hand while his outside fingers carry the melody notes. An unexpected alignment of ten notes ends the piece abruptly.

"Thank you. . . ." He taps the microphone and then slaps it lightly with three fingers. Is it on? "Thank you, ladies and gentlemen. . . ." A deep voice, followed by more tapping. "Thank you, ladies and gentlemen, and good evening to you. Now Butch Warren will play a bass solo for you." Monk goes hurriedly off the stand with a couple of right and left lunging movements that seem to contradict each other but which end him up on the patio behind the bandstand.

Warren plays a cleanly articulated *Softly, as in a Morning Sunrise*. As he begins, Charlie Rouse arrives and ducks quickly behind the bandstand. Monk paces erratically.

"And now Frankie Dunlop will warm up with a number."

About two minutes later, Monk and Warren are back on the bandstand, and Monk offers his brittle, out-of-tempo opening chorus to *I'm Getting Sentimental over You*. Just before the bridge, Monk leans to his left and looks under the piano, almost as if the next notes were down there somewhere. Then a break takes them into tempo for the second chorus, with tenor saxophonist Rouse walking onto the bandstand as he plays, and Monk really working behind him with a clipped distillation of the melody in support.

Halfway through the chorus, Monk gets up, leaving his instrument to undertake his swaying, shuffling dance. Half the crowd seems to be nodding knowingly about his eccentricity. But a few in the audience seem to realize that, besides giving the group a change of texture and sound by laying out, Monk is conducting. His movements are encouraging drummer Dunlop and Warren, particularly, to hear, not just the obvious beat, but the accent and space *around* the one-two-three-four, the rhythms that Monk is so interested in.

Warren solos, and Monk and Rouse leave the stand. Then Dunlop is there alone. He articulates the four eight-bar divisions of the piece very clearly on his drums for two choruses. The group reassembles. Anybody who can't dig the music will probably like the show.

Monk's well-known bass figure leads him to a fast *Epistrophy*, his theme. They give it a full performance. Monk accompanies Rouse with accents that are dazzling, although he isn't playing so demandingly on his theme. Then he signals musically for Rouse to come back for the out chorus.

Midnight. The piece ends; the set is over. Monk leads the way off the stand, and for a moment the piano sits empty, in an amber spotlight.

At the door, two couples arrive and ask, "When will Monk be on again?"

"He should be back in an hour. Roland Hanna will be on in a few minutes."

"You wanna wait? You wanna go in now or come back?"

Recording with "Bags"

Even with its daily wrap-around line of attending tourists, New York's Radio City Music Hall does not look much like a movie palace. It looks even less like a recording studio, but if you go through the stage entrance, take an elevator to the seventh floor, climb up a flight of stairs, and pass through a couple of unmarked green doors, you will find yourself at Plaza Sound, a large recording studio, well equipped and well cared for (there is a good piano, and it is kept in tune), that is usually used by, among others, Riverside records.

Riverside booked Plaza's facilities on an afternoon in spring to record one of its more illustrious contractees, vibraharpist Milt Jackson.

Jackson is perhaps known as the most immediately compelling player in the Modern Jazz Quartet. He has also been successfully making records on his own for years, with groups small and large. On this occasion

Jackson was to record with a brass orchestra of four trumpets, three trombones, tuba, three French horns, and a rhythm section. To do the scoring, there was Melba Liston, a brass player herself (a trombonist) as well as arranger (she has worked with the bands of Dizzy Gillespie, Count Basie, and Quincy Jones), and perhaps the only woman to make her way successfully in the strange subculture of modern-jazz record dates and public performances. For that matter, she is one of the few women instrumentalists and composers to make her way successfully in any kind of jazz.

The date was called for 1 P.M., but several of the players had arrived early, among them pianist Hank Jones, drummer Charlie Persip, and trombonists Jimmy Cleveland and Quentin Jackson. Also present was trumpeter Clark Terry, who had, in the parlance of the American Federation of Musicians, "contracted" the date; that is, he had assembled the specific players to fit Miss Liston's instrumentation.

Terry is also in effect a constantly alert concert-master—he holds run-throughs of difficult parts and helps to revise scoring as needed. On this occasion, he was to act as a responsible and humorous buffer between a quiet-spoken Miss Liston and a sometimes talkative group of players.

Milt Jackson himself already was setting up his vibraharp, with the help of an assistant, and picking out his mallets. Jackson is a small, thin man, and he is usually cheerfully quiet—indeed, it is as if Jackson usually says something only if he absolutely has to. But today as he worked, he was chatting freely and constantly with Jones and Terry. Perhaps the introverted Milt Jackson was becoming as extroverted as his music.

By 12:50 P.M., the studio was abustle with greetings. In a corner two trumpeters were in a serious discussion of the relative merits of mouthpieces.

At 12:55 P.M., a door at the far end of the studio swung open and in walked Melba Liston, to be greeted by an enthusiastic burst of "Melbos!" from Jackson and an elliptical "What know, Melba?" from Terry. Miss Liston, a pleasant, handsome woman of medium height, was dressed in a dark skirt and a salmon-colored leather jacket. She carried two evidences of her dual position in life: a handbag and a briefcase containing her scores.

Almost on her heels entered Orrin Keepnews, A & R man for Riverside and producer of the date. Sporting a recently reshaped Van Dyke beard and a meerschaum pipe, Keepnews wended his way across the studio, nodding briefly to the small group of visitors and wives near the door. He shook hands with Hank Jones, spoke to some of the musicians, and then entered the studio booth to take his place beside Riverside's engineer, Ray Fowler.

By this time, all the players had arrived save one, trumpeter Thad Jones; he had been mistaken about the hour of the date but was now on his way. The room was a lively buzz of talk, and everyone seemed eager to go to work. It was decided to get in some rehearsal of the arrangements until Thad arrived. The brass was seated on a raised platform facing Miss

Liston, and to her left Jackson and the rhythm formed a kind of semicircle. Milt crossed to Melba, picked up his part, glanced at it, looked up at her, said with an enigmatic half-smile, "Hard! I knew that," and crossed back over to his instrument.

An almost uncanny aspect of any jazz record date is the ability of the players to accomplish several things at once—some casual, some trivial, some genial, some noisy, some exacting, some serious. And now, as Terry helped Miss Liston distribute the parts among the players, Jackson and Hank Jones held a conversation on the various types of address books they had used, Jackson discussed his coming tour with the Modern Jazz Quartet, Jones sounded an A for the brass to tune up to, and both managed to gain an idea of what music they would be playing for the next four hours by glancing casually at Miss Liston's scores.

In deference to the nominal leader and star of the date, Melba said to Milt, "Shall we run down the blues?"

And the star, not so much in deference to his arranger as in the statement of a man who is usually ready to play anything any time, as long as he is playing, said, "I don't care."

So the arranger said to the orchestra, "Get out the minor blues." As they did, she instructed, above their muffled but continuing conversation, "This is a very soft, light thing," all the time snapping her fingers quietly and slowly to indicate the tempo.

"Ready, horns?" But they weren't. There was still

some sporadic tuning up, so she held up a bit longer. Then she started them in a slow, muted transmutation of Jackson's basic blues theme, known in its classic version as *Bags' Groove*. (Bags, Jackson's nickname, supposedly derives from his appearance after several sleepless Detroit nights spent in celebration of his Army discharge in the mid-Forties—but anyone who has seen him without his glasses knows that the nickname might have been appointed any time, for his eyes nearly always look bagged.)

After one chorus of *Bags' Minor Blues*, several players made the collective mistake of slipping into major. Unexpectedly, it was Jackson who stopped them with, "Well, is this minor or not?"

A spontaneous, "Hey, Bags!" came from somewhere in the middle of the group. This interjection might have implied, "Well, so *you're* taking charge. . . . That's sort of new. Before, you might have looked surprised at a thing like this but let somebody else do the correcting. You're right—we goofed. But we like you in this new role. . . ."

This had all sunk in immediately, and Jackson had moved over by Hank Jones and was showing him an apparently hilarious mistake that the music copyist had made on his part. That part, it should be noted, like most jazz soloists' parts, consisted of a few written ensemble figures and long stretches of chord symbols, within which harmonic framework the player is to improvise.

On a second try, they finished the piece, and its opening gentleness proved to be contrasted, about halfway through, in a sudden shout of brass encouragement. On that shout, Jackson—arms flying even in a run-through—rode to a further ad lib variation. Then the opening delicacy was restored by horns and vibes at the balanced ending of the piece.

Jackson: "Is that what I'm supposed to play at the end?"

Miss Liston: "Whatever you like."

The French horns, meanwhile, were running over a short section among themselves.

Jackson: "When they have those eight bars *forte*, what am I supposed to do? Go on playing right through? Yeah, I am?"

He seemed shyly surprised and delighted at the idea.

Miss Liston turned to the group and said, "Right there break it on the third beat. Do-do-lit-do-*wah!*"

As they ran the piece through again, she did no timekeeping but conducted only the dynamics and the feeling she wanted by an expressive pantomime: closing her eyes, moving her hands delicately in the air, swaying slightly, and tilting and turning her head to the sound of the music.

At the end Terry said, "We can make that rot now."

"Rot now?" countered Jackson as they both laughed.

But as if to correct himself, Terry turned to the trumpeters and indicated a section of the score with, "Let's try that part at letter E again."

Then they worked on something called *Bossa Bags*.

Jackson joked that he was sure that the bossa nova had to be on the way out by now, and Terry countered that it couldn't be just yet because he had only recently made one. But even a slight indication on Jackson's part that he might be concerned with what could make a hit record seemed a new concern for him to be voicing.

Thad Jones arrived, took some kidding about the reasons for his tardiness, and quickly participated in a second run-through of *Bossa Bags*. The score wasn't easy, and at one point Hank Jones succeeded in smoothing a minor disagreement between two of the horn men by amusingly underlining their verbal exchange with threatening silent-movie tremolos.

"I'm gonna scratch the intro and let the rhythm take it," Melba announced to an unresponsive din. Then louder: "Scratch the intro!"

"Then what about a drum solo?" Persip asked quietly. But he was already joining piano and bass in working out a new beginning. They worked it up quickly, but as Keepnews called through the studio loudspeaker for them to try recording a first take of the piece, Terry and Miss Liston had their heads together, revising the ending according to an idea Terry had.

The group memorized the new conclusion quickly, and in a few minutes engineer Fowler was reading "Session No. 156, Reel 1, Take 1" onto the rolling recording tape, and after one brief false start, the first take had begun.

During the performance, everyone looked deadly

serious and strictly business until Jackson's eyes bobbed up at the end of his solo. He was smiling, as usual. He always seems pleasantly surprised when an improvisation comes off well.

The take was played back—chiefly to check matters of recording balance—and the conversation gradually buzzed up in the studio. It was, after all, only the first take, and first takes are usually technical things.

The new Milt Jackson entered the engineer's booth briefly to tell Keepnews that he had decided the minor blues did not have the sort of commercial potential for a release on a 45-rpm single. So they might as well expand the arrangement with improvised choruses by some of the trumpeters.

Then the old Milt Jackson played a fine solo as they tried another take of *Bossa Bags*.

Immediately, Terry requested "one more take right away," sensing that the psychological moment for a really good version of the piece was imminent.

As they played, Hank Jones's feet danced away under the piano, Jackson leaned attentively over his instrument, and, at the finish, the brass men smiled.

As the reverberations drifted off, Miss Liston called out to the booth, "Let's hear that one!"

She seemed casually confident as the playback began to fill the studio, even joining drummer Persip in a brief dance. She was listening carefully, though, and toward the end stopped abruptly, having heard one wrong note from the eleven instruments. From the middle of the orchestra the culprit, one of the French horn players, immediately confessed.

"We'll put it in the liner notes that he played a wrong note," Jackson cracked.

The rest of the take, however, had been good, and they could briefly lift the passage in question from a previous take and splice it in. So much for *Bossa Bags*.

It was time for a slow ballad, the sort of piece that Jackson's natural earthiness can transform so brilliantly. As Terry and Miss Liston passed out the copies of *Flamingo*, Jackson and Hank Jones were already kidding the introduction with a few overripe trills, as if to clear the piece of any latent sentimentality.

The run-through suggested that Miss Liston had done some of her writing in Jackson's style, but simpler, so as to underline the kind of thing he would improvise. It worked effectively. The run-through also revealed a great deal of muted work for the trumpeters and a need for supplementary tympani. This meant that Fowler had to move some of his mikes in closer to the horns and that Persip had to assemble and tune up some new equipment. Jackson, meanwhile, was obviously eager to play again. And Terry, as usual, was running down a few rough spots with the horns.

"Let's go from the top," said Melba.

"Matter of fact, we could try one if you like," said Terry.

"Okay, let's see how it sounds."

But the opening proved to be tough, and they decided that as soon as they got a good version, they could hold it and splice it onto a good performance of the rest of the piece. (Ah, the joys of tape!)

The tempo was especially slow, creating a mood hard to sustain if everyone isn't playing well. Jackson's solo moved from wild, double-time embellishments of the theme to simply bluesy melodies—and back again, contrast upon contrast. With eyebrows raised, he faced his vibraharp fiercely and then bent over it abruptly, his arms and hands always moving above and around its keyboard. It was as if he had to coerce warmth and melody out of so cold and metallic an instrument. Many vibists take an easy way out by settling for a simple, appealing percussiveness, but Jackson is always a passionate melodist. Still, he is never without his humor, and at one point when he apparently felt the trumpets were playing with a bit too much schmaltz, he tossed them back such obvious musical schmaltz that they came off it immediately.

"Did the copyist make some mistakes in there—are there any wrong notes?" suggested someone over a loudspeaker from the booth.

"No," said Melba. "That's part of the sound I want."

"See," said Jackson, smiling an aside to Fowler, who was in the studio raising a microphone, "she wrote that in."

Meanwhile, the arranger had moved into the control booth to give her full attention to a playback of the last take. She was retreating not only from the usual conversation in the studio, but also from the fact that it had been increased by the arrival of a messenger from a nearby delicatessen carrying a heavy load of coffee and doughnuts.

She stood with her back to the loudspeakers and her eyes shut, taking in the music. Sometimes she sang quietly along with the brass, sometimes she only swayed with it. The expression on her face was a kaleidoscope of passion, pain, release, and finally, peace. During the solos she waited politely attentive; during the closing ensemble passages she closed her eyes again, raised her hands in delicate movement, and, at the end, smiled without comment. Then, still moved, she turned to Keepnews and said something that sounded like "t-tttt-th-th-t."

"Sure" he said, understandingly, "we can fade out the ending gradually."

A wise leader saves a twelve-bar blues for the moment in the record date when spirits begin to flag, for playing the blues can lift them. And now Melba suggested they record *Bags' Minor Blues*, expanded with solo choruses by the trumpets.

"You'll see why I got A to play his solo before B," Keepnews was saying in the booth. "If I didn't, B might just coast through some of his clichés."

It worked apparently, for B played a very good chorus.

A couple more takes were done, and Jackson came into the booth, asking Keepnews if the last one was okay. Keepnews agreed it was and when Jackson had left, remarked, "A year ago he would have just left it up to me or Melba and said nothing. I wish I had the first date I did with him to do all over again, now that his shyness is gone."

Back in the studio, someone had distributed W-2 forms, the income-tax withholding slips, and the musicians were filling them in, a sign that the date was over.

In a few minutes they were into the final number, a superior but little-known ballad by Buddy Johnson called *Save Your Love for Me*. They made it on the third try. Persip's brushes made a faintly broken whisper across his snare drums. Jimmy Cleveland chewed gum at a wildly fast tempo between his slowly delivered trombone phrases. In the middle, Jackson abruptly bent over his instrument for a ringing cascade of notes and smiled broadly at the cleanly executed shaking brass crescendo that answered him. He began his delicate solo section in double-time, and the bass, piano, and drums went with him immediately by a kind of collective intuition.

Melba was almost swirling with the tempo. Then she raised her arms to signal a return to the lyric quietude with which the piece had begun, and the last notes rang out.

At the end, "Magnifique!" Terry exclaimed.

"Play it back, and then we'll go home," Keepnews said to Fowler in the booth in complete agreement.

RECORD NOTE

The recordings made at this session were issued on Riverside RLP 478/9478.

Big Joe in the Studio

The blues revival—the sudden renaissance of interest in the so-called "country blues" singers—is one of the most singular events in the history of American recordings. One company set up a subsidiary label to handle releases by these nearly legendary American bards, calling it Bluesville (which is pretty hip, you must admit). Another called its label Bluesway. Still another, which originally added some modern jazz LPs to its line as money-makers, soon found the blues men supporting the horn men. And singers who once had a few 78 rpm singles on the market, primarily intended for sales in Negro neighborhoods in big cities, now find themselves with several forty-minute LPs, primarily bought by a white audience, a white audience now thoroughly acquainted with blues-derived rock and roll.

There have been a few hypes and a few deceptions in this activity. One performer, spoken of in reverent tones as "one of the all-time greats" by younger record collectors, turns out to be a dull old man who has endless sets of humorless dirty verses, set to three borrowed melodies which he uses over and over. Another man, with a far more interesting style and approach, can actually perform only about four numbers, and for encores monotonously reshuffles the same material. Big Bill Broonzy became the toast of several European cities by slowing down some of his old urban jump numbers on the woes of wooing and passing them off as authentically archaic country blues. He interspersed them with folk songs he learned off other people's records and told wonderful old stories between songs. Of course, the remarkable thing about Big Bill was that, for all the deliberateness with which he was putting the world on with this country-boy act, he remained a powerful and strangely honest performer.

But the blues revival has been responsible for some wonderful rediscoveries and renewed careers. One of these belongs to Joe Lee Williams, "Big Joe" Williams. Big Joe sings now as he did in the Twenties and Thirties—he has not changed his style, his approach, his speed, or his repertory one bit, and he is a powerful, moving, humorous, forceful blues man. Big Joe is his own man, and I doubt if he could be anything else or that it would ever occur to him to try. For the record I should add that of course I do not speak of the other Joe Williams who is primarily a ballad singer but who did a lot of popular blues numbers with Count Basie during the mid-Fifties.

Big Joe Williams is a stocky man of medium height

and, except when he is singing, he has an almost reticent personality. He was born in 1903, on October 16, in Crawford, Mississippi—the heart of the blues country, the area, some singers say with pride, where the blues first came from longer ago than anyone living can remember. His grandfather sang hymns and played the accordion, and even knew some blues. There were cousins who played washboard ("could make it talk") and guitar and sang. A brother and another cousin did spirituals and gospel songs. The house was full of music, made by the people who lived there. And when he was quite young, Joe Williams decided that he didn't want to pick cotton or plow, fashioned his own instrument out of some wire, sticks, and spools, and soon set out to become a singer. He toured the South in the shows that had the likes of Ethel Waters in top billing, and was soon making records on his own. Beginning in 1935, he was constantly in print on 78 rpms, and he did not lose that fame until the mid-Forties, when the urban "rhythm and blues" style made him unfashionable. But he has endured, and recently he was sitting in a New York recording studio, getting ready to cut for a major jazz label to prove it. Prove it he did.

Big Joe had suddenly presented himself via the telephone to Kenny Goldstein of Prestige Records. "I wanted to record him and we had some plans for later," says Goldstein, "but he all of a sudden showed up in New York. He called me and said, 'I'm here now at the Hotel Teresa. I got rolled of $175, so can we do the record now?' I had the Cue recording studios lined up the next day for a folk-music date, so I just called up the folk singers, canceled them out, and booked in Big Joe."

Things got started at Cue studios about 12:30 in the afternoon. Big Joe had come in, looking serious and slightly worried. He was dressed in a pair of brown trousers which had long since lost their crease and he had on a flannel shirt in which he might have traveled quite a distance. Behind the glass panel of the recording booth were Goldstein, poring over his logs and notes, and Cue's engineer, Mel Kaiser, threading his tape machines and preparing to enter the studio and place his microphones to pick up the music. Inside the small studio room itself, Big Joe began replacing a broken string in his battered guitar, a personally doctored instrument to which he has added three extra strings. From the end of that ancient instrument ran an electric cord which attached it to an even more battered amplifier. On one side of the amplifier box was a pair of dice drawn with white paint. On the other was lettered "BIG JOE." But as Joe Williams installed and tuned up his new guitar string it became obvious that this wreck of an amplifier had the expressive sound that he wanted and that, although their standards might not be the same, Joe was as careful in his way about tuning his guitar as a virtuoso violinist might be about his Stradivarius.

In the studio with Joe was the tall and heavy-set Chicago bass player, Willie Dixon, who shows up on about a third of the blues record dates made these days. Joe had also asked for a harmonica to accompany him. He wanted those very special plaintive wails and abrupt, guttural comments that only the "harp," as the blues men call it, can provide. For his harp man Goldstein, with the help of writer Pete Welding, had—remarkably—come up with a man only twenty-two years old named Larry Johnson. Johnson, who works as a superintendent in a Bronx apartment house, plays a kind of authentically wailing, back-country harmonica that would not have seemed out of place on a blues record made in 1927. "I come from down Georgia and I can play country harp," he announced. "You'll see."

"I used to sing down there in Georgia," said Big Joe, recalling the Twenties. "And I recorded there with Barbecue Bob, for Paramount," he added in his usual hurried speech, which is slightly slurred nowadays by a couple of missing teeth.

Joe Williams constantly adjusted and turned his strings as he spoke. Then, pointing to a heavily smoking ashtray on a nearby studio table, he said abruptly to Johnson, "Put that cigarette out." Then, with a kind of half-smile, "I'm tough on harp players."

To the rear of the room, Willie Dixon announced he was ready to go by taking off his shirt, and then began testing his bass. He was tuning it up to the sound of Big Joe's guitar in a way that might not get approval in a concert hall but was deliberate and quite effective nevertheless. Dixon looked casual and seemed only half-concerned; Big Joe was absolutely serious and seemed only half-confident.

"You know this piece?" young Johnson was saying to Dixon as he ran off a blues melody on his harp.

Dixon nodded, unconcerned. "And how about this one?" Johnson played another.

"Don't play them other things, please," said Joe. "I don't want to get other people's numbers in my head now, you know. I got to remember my own."

Joe had now decided to warm up for real, and it was soon obvious that he was also testing the abilities of the other two men—especially Johnson's. To a man like Big Joe Williams, tempo, speed, is especially important. Although their melodies may differ, most of his pieces are more or less in three basic blues forms, but the different speeds at which he does them carry meaning in themselves.

He began with an easy one, a medium tempo. It is easier for a group to swing collectively and keep up a beat at medium speed. Then he set a harder test, a slower tempo. He was teasing them—could they keep the momentum without leaning on the beat?

So far Joe hadn't sung a note that mattered, although he was tossing out a few traditional verses as they went along. There was one old verse—it must have been very old, for it was about a farmer's cow, and not about a woman or a train as most later blues are. But even in such casual use, Joe's voice, its sound and its emotional impact, took complete possession of the room and everyone in it; this formerly unprepossessing man became an intense and commanding presence. If he could move one nearly to tears in an offhand rehearsal, what would this suddenly authoritative singer do when the tapes were rolling and the session was really under way?

The players had passed the slow test, so Joe started in on a little boogie-woogie figure which took them into a very fast blues. Could they maintain the pace? Dixon and Johnson wailed and jumped and swung along with it until Joe was satisfied they could. Then, the final test—and Joe was really getting down to business with this one; it was a *very* slow blues, the kind that loses all drive when handled by technical or emotional amateurs. It went so well that Dixon was quite wrapped up in his playing at the end. And Johnson, for a moment, seemed quite wrapped up in himself because of the unspoken approval he was getting.

"How long is that ending, Big Joe? Do you know how many bars it's going to be?"

"Might be different different times. Just you follow along." Joe didn't say it but he is apt to skip a few bars now and then when he gets going. The other men had to keep their ears open and follow him in that too, and they did. Young Johnson was getting in the mood, and probably thinking of all the legendary stories about the durability of blues men. "You-all gonna play somewhere tonight?" he asked Big Joe and Dixon. Joe smiled, "Time we get through here, we'll be pretty tired out." Clay feet. The younger man seemed surprised and disappointed; he lost himself in tuning up his various harmonicas, trying them out with the sound of Joe's guitar, quickly switching around from one to another of the several sizes, shapes, and tunings he had brought with him.

Now they were really down to business. Joe was

recording a piece he began, "Oh, yeah, my baby don't love me no more," and the small studio swayed in attention. By the end of it everybody had looked up but Joe, for in the booth, smiling shrewdly through the glass panel, was a rather illustrious visitor—Peter Chatman, professionally "Memphis Slim," pianist, singer, and one of the most successful participants in the current blues revival. Slim is a tall, imposing figure, and a slyly humorous man. At the end of the piece, he quickly slipped into the studio, getting greetings from all assembled as he crossed to the piano. Almost immediately Big Joe got the floor back. "This is what we're going to do next," he said, striking a figure on his guitar as Johnson joined him.

"What key you in?" Slim addressed Dixon, raising the corner of his mouth and one eyebrow. Dixon shrugged without turning around, and kept playing.

At the end of the run-through, there was again too much small talk for Big Joe, and this time he laid down a law. "Everybody quiet now, 'cause when I'm cutting a record I get mad! I don't want no talking or laughing."

"Do you want me to holler 'Play it Joe' when you take your guitar solo?" It was Slim, of course, from across the room. And what could Joe do but smile and say reluctantly, "Yeah, that'll be all right."

Now they were listening to a playback of Big Joe's *38 Pistol Blues*. Most blues men have a version of the pistol piece. Joe heard his line about " 'Way down lovers lane" with a smile, and then grinned with approval as his guitar solo went into double-timing and the train whistle effects at the end. The others were amused too. "If I didn't play that ending, it wouldn't be Big Joe Williams. I started that many years ago."

As the conversation in the studio began to buzz up again, he reminded them, "I don't wanna get my mind on that talk, just on the records."

Soon they were into another take, *Pearly Mae*, a blues with verses about young love that probably go back to a British or Irish folk ballad. But to Joe, his guitar, filling in between the verses, says as much as the words themselves. "Now, look here baby," he spoke quietly in the middle of the piece to introduce his solo, the heart of the matter. Then he sang the ending, "I ain't had no proper lovin' . . ./Please bring your pearls back home." Nobody seemed to want to hear a playback at the end of that one, it had gone so well, so Joe began to work on the next piece. He had provided Dixon with some wrinkled sheets of paper, reminders of his own numbers, and the bassist was reading to him aloud, "Just a fool about my baby/But she don't care nothin' about me."

Memphis Slim was not going to let up. From inside the control booth, where he had moved beside Goldstein, he began announcing over the loudspeakers, "Now Joe, you've just got to smile more. We were thinking about making a movie of this." But in the studio, Joe was concentrating too hard on Dixon's reading to pay much attention. Joe also didn't hear the remark of one visitor across the room, "If you sent this guy to London, he'd kill those people over there —just don't let him change that red shirt."

They got *Just a Fool About My Baby* onto the tapes in one easy attempt, and Joe remembered all the words. Then they went into a fast shuffle boogie number which Joe calls *Skinny Mama*, and Big Joe smiled all the way through it as he played and sang, just the way the music smiles. The rapport between Dixon and Big Joe is almost telepathic. They were rocking now, and the officials, the visitors, and even the studio walls seem to be rocking with them.

One after another, Joe's numbers went onto the tape now with no retakes. "*Walkin' Blues*, next!" Joe announced.

That done, "Let's do my jump." It turned out to be a personal variant of the salacious old song most singers call the *Jockey Blues*. ("My gal's a jockey, she's teaching me how to ride," goes the more usual version. "She says once in the middle and twice on either side.") Slim knew the piece differently and apparently didn't approve of Joe's performance because he muttered something about, "He got his horse mixed up with his mule."

"Well," a visitor turned to him smiling, "last week I heard about a man who had three record dates, for three different companies. He did the same bunch of numbers on each one, just switched the titles and the words around a little bit."

"I like you too," said Slim, eyeing the speaker shrewdly.

Three hours later, Joe had twenty-one musical numbers all on tape, more than enough for two LPs. He had brought the words to twenty with him, but he had dropped a few and had remembered more as he went along.

Earlier, Goldstein had decided to call one of the albums *"Blues for Twenty-Seven Strings,"* and to ask Joe to play a twelve-string guitar on some of the pieces. Joe now turned to the more complex instrument, tuned it, tried a few effects, and was pleased with what he got. "How you like that twelve-string sound?" he asked the room in general. "Good, ain't it?"

They recorded *Sugar Baby* and Johnson's playing seemed to be too loud for Big Joe. At first he tried lowering his voice to see if his accompanist would take the hint and bring himself down a bit. It didn't quite work. Then Joe ad-libbed a verse about, "Don't like the way you do." It could have been part of the song, but it was also a direct instruction to Larry Johnson. On the playback he pointed to it.

"You hear that, Larry? I sang that for you." And then, "Yeah, listen to that twelve-string guitar talking."

"That *is* a good instrument. Listen to those sounds," young Johnson agreed.

Then it was Joe's time again. "That's not in the guitar. It's in the man!"

RECORD NOTE

Big Joe Williams has LPs on Arhoolie, Folkways, and Delmar, as well as Prestige/Bluesville.

Jimmy Giuffre at Home

Jimmy Giuffre's music sometimes involves the sort of
improvisation that is called by that graceless and
ambiguous name, the "new thing." And like many
musicians working on such free and spontaneous
playing, Giuffre rehearses often. It is partly a matter
of keeping himself and his music well practiced, of
course, and of trying out new pieces. But it is also a
matter of personal pleasure and of aesthetic adventure,
for Giuffre and his associates are discovering a new
musical idiom. Each rehearsal will probably fulfill
new possibilities for the music, rejecting some approaches and affirming or suggesting others.

Giuffre's original companions when he undertook
"free" improvisation included pianist Paul Bley and
bassist Steve Swallow. Their work did produce some
grumbling that the sometimes moody and out-of-
strict-tempo performances they offered begged comparison with modern written chamber music. Ornette

Coleman's "free" music *sounded* like jazz, it was said, but Giuffre's somehow did not. On the other hand, only jazz musicians could play with the sort of immediacy that the Giuffre trio offers, or would use their instruments with such exploratory daring, or would be able to improvise so well.

By mid-1964, if Swallow was not available, Gary Peacock would rehearse as the Giuffre bassist, and Don Friedman had become the group's pianist. Subsequently, many other players have participated, among them bassists Cecil McBee, Richard Davis, and Barre Phillips; pianists Don Pullen and Bob James; and, on those occasions when the trio has become a quartet, drummers Andrew Cyrille, Milford Graves, Joe Hunt, Joe Chambers, and others.

Peacock had fitted into this music almost from the beginning, and before Bley's departure. And from the first time Don Friedman made a session, both he and Giuffre knew that the pianist's response to the idiom was exceptional.

It is gratifying to discover how many young players can contribute to a free and challenging idiom like Giuffre's, a music which does away with traditional melody forms and traditional harmonic and rhythmic guideposts and makes heavy demands for unpremeditated invention on the player.

Jimmy and Juanita Giuffre's apartment is on the upper east side of New York City. It is the kind New Yorkers call a "railroad flat," meaning that the five small, neat rooms are strung out one after the other, that there is no hallway, and one room leads directly into the next. The front room has a Steinway grand and is the music room. Two rooms to the rear is Jimmy's study, with a tape recorder that usually figures as an important part of rehearsing.

Wednesday afternoons are usually rehearsal times, and on a Wednesday in February 1964 Giuffre, Friedman, and Peacock gathered to try a new extended piece called *Trio in Flux*.

The first to arrive out of the cold, slushy New York streets is Gary Peacock. He is wearing a duffle coat, a dark blue lightweight suit, and overshoes. Peacock was unable to bring his own bass along, and planned to use a discarded and disrepaired instrument that Swallow leaves at the Giuffre place.

As he takes off his coat and places his wet overshoes on a piece of newspaper near the front door Gary offers energetic greetings, which Giuffre returns in quiet Texan speech, suggesting "coffee or something." The bassist replies that he would like a "coffee royal" and proceeds to give the recipe. Giuffre moves to the kitchen and takes down a small aluminum coffee pot, while Peacock moves to the front room to inspect Swallow's bass. A few minutes later Friedman arrives, removes an overcoat, a tweed jacket, and a pair of slush-laden fur-lined boots, leaving himself in button-down shirt, grey flannel trousers, and black socks. Soon the trio is sitting around the Giuffres' kitchen table variously sipping coffee, tea, and (for Friedman) a small glass of water. After a quota of news and small talk, someone says, "Well, let's play."

Without another word the three men move to the music room.

As they take their places, Giuffre begins to comment on *Trio in Flux*. It is a piece in five parts, each introduced by a written section, and lasting, in performance, roughly fifteen minutes. The opening and closing parts are for the full trio; the second part is a duo for bass and piano; the third is a duo for clarinet and bass; the fourth for clarinet and piano.

Thus all the combinations and textures for the trio are explored. The score is marked "no tempo (moderate)," and no steady tempo should be set up in performance—the player tries to let each of his musical phrases find its own best tempo.

As with most of the Giuffre Trio's current pieces, the themes don't set up chord structures on which to improvise and don't necessarily establish keys or modes for the players to improvise in. The written part suggests musical ideas—moods, if you will— upon which the players build their melodies. Furthermore, although one player may predominate for a given moment, all three are equal melodic participants, and the music is a collective melodic effort as it unfolds.

However, *Trio in Flux* has a further aspect: even in the written parts, the players take the phrases one at a time, each man playing off each of his lines as he feels it. Each man should listen to the others, and make his part fit in properly, and no player should get too far ahead or behind. Thus the written parts of the piece will also sound different in each performance.

"It is like three actors, three comedians," Giuffre explains. "Each man knows his own lines and his own movements. But each time they work, each man has to hear the others and allow for their lines and movements, and each allows for the special timing of the others. For instance, in playing my one phrase here [he points to the score] I allow the piano part to come off before I go into my next phrase here. But one time Don may not play this as fast or slow as the next time or give the notes exactly the same kind of accents, so my pause and response will be different each time too. Stretch or condense as you want to.

"First, let's work on the written parts, and we'll improvise later."

The musicians begin. As they play the first section, three interdependent lines seem to be moving in an enormous musical space. The movements of the lines are personal, but each responds to the other.

At the end, Giuffre, who has been standing in the curve of the piano, turns to Friedman.

"Just to pick on you a little about the last part," he says and moves toward the keyboard and Friedman's music sheet, "I think it would be better if you break these phrases up with more space in between them."

Friedman nods.

"Hey," says Peacock, raising his instrument, "I think I'm scratching up your floor with this bass."

"I've got something," says Giuffre, and he heads for the rear of the apartment, returning with a small throw rug which he and Peacock place on the floor under the bass.

They play the opening section again. It is familiar, yet different.

"That was perfect," says Giuffre. "I would say, let that last note lay there for a long time. Now let's go to the next part."

It is for Friedman and Peacock and is like a discourse, with Friedman asserting high notes and Peacock replying with "yes, but . . ." notes from below. Then the argument reverses, with Peacock moving upward, Friedman downward. At the end, Peacock's instrument reverberates.

"This has to be very strong," says Giuffre, pointing to Peacock's part. "That G-flat has to ring with everything you've got."

The duo starts again as Giuffre moves into the next room to catch the balance of the two instruments.

"What do you have in the third bar?" Friedman asks the bassist, apparently puzzled by what he has heard.

The two men play the section again. As its last notes hang in the air, they seem to plead for the improvisation that would normally extend and finally resolve the written section.

Next, the duo for clarinet and bass.

"Keep the drive up without going into a steady tempo," says Giuffre after the first try. And again, "Good, but can you do it just a little slower, because my part needs stretching out. No, wait—that sounds in tempo. It sounds like quarter notes."

They try it again, and Giuffre pronounces it good: "Once more and we've got it."

The next section is for piano and clarinet, and after they have run it through once, Giuffre says, "It's working out well, but you were just a bar ahead of me. The good thing is that we were working together so that the audience could hear everything each of us does. There's no part being wasted."

Friedman's bass notes are moving upward now. Giuffre re-enters high. At the end, he lowers his clarinet, smiling, "I beat you out that time. But that doesn't matter, of course."

Peacock looks at Giuffre, saying, "The idea is to get each part to have its own movement."

"Yes, I don't want it to be symmetrical horizontally. Okay, Letter E. This part here"—he holds up his part to the others—"is very complex, so we will stretch it out."

About a third of the way in, Peacock plays a wrong note, emits a heavy groan, and follows it by a Bronx cheer. Laughter by the three then assents to a new start.

"The pace you play at is your own, plus what the other guys are doing—I just think of giving it movement," Giuffre says to the room in general, gesturing with a sweep of his right arm. Then he turns to Friedman and continues, "Gary's got the most busy part in this." Peacock solicits Friedman's help in tuning up the slightly seamy bass, after which he begins working on his part.

Soon Friedman says, "Let's try Letter E again."

Giuffre agrees with "Take some time on these cadenzas." They begin, Giuffre playing with loose fingering and loose embouchure to get the sound he wants. Suddenly he stops in mid-phrase.

"Hey! My horn fell out of my mouth," he says with a laugh. "You know that happened to me onstage once."

They begin once more. "No, wait!" It is Giuffre, laughing again. "I was trying to play your part." He is looking up at Peacock.

The ending is played with such unity that Friedman's smiling notes seem to echo inside Peacock's bass, and Peacock's broad sound inside the piano's sounding board.

"Now," says Giuffre. "I think we've got that, so let's try it all the way with the, ahem. . . ." He pauses, coughs officiously, and then says very carefully, smiling, "Im-provi-ZA-tion."

As Peacock scat-sings a fragment of his part to try it rhythmically, Giuffre heads toward the tape recorder. He has a second thought, however, and returns, saying, "I remember this now—during the duets, the other fellow could add some color, from the theme material maybe, while the other two are improvising. But not if it sounds contrived. A figure maybe."

There is some discussion of the idea, and Peacock suggests, "Maybe I should play something pianistic or clarinetish."

"No. Maybe just a phrase if it fits, but your own. Well, let's do a version of it on the tape, and see what happens."

Giuffre moves back to the recorder to switch it on. Then he announces, for the benefit of the microphone, *"Trio in Flux"*—and then laughs: "Trio influx —too many trios."

The opening is sharp and strong. Giuffre hits a long note, making it more than one by loosening his embouchure and sounding its overtones. (He has written it in the score: "overtones, loosen embouchure.") In the improvising, Friedman takes off in a humorous flutter of notes, and Giuffre scurries behind him in imitation. Then they are both into strong melodies in the middle register. Next Giuffre darts high, then low. And at one point Friedman augments a strong chord with the additional sound of the clap of the piano top as he slams it back into place.

Friedman not only lets each piano phrase move with its own rhythm and momentum, separate from the next, and without benefit of a steady tempo, but he can let each phrase swing with real jazz rhythm. That capacity and his open wit fit this music excellently.

Giuffre gradually diminishes a note into silence, and they all know the section is over. A pause. Then Peacock leads into the next section for piano and bass. Here the busy improvisation takes on an intermittent third part, shared equally by Peacock's occasional percussive sounds thumped on the side of his bass and Friedman's discreet manipulation of his piano top. A little bit of overdoing, and these effects might become grim or even ridiculous, of course, but the two handle them with musical taste and feeling. Then the bassist uses his bow, and Friedman occasionally strums the piano strings with his fingers and fingernails as new sounds and textures emerge.

Suddenly there is a disruptive, flapping sound as the tape runs off in the next room. Giuffre rushes in, turns off the machine, and is back for the last notes of the duo.

They are into the last session, with all three men participating. All the lines are still clear and independent but interrelated. Peacock's sustained final note and Friedman's reverberations finish it.

"Everybody ready to hear that?" the leader asks, moving toward the tape recorder in the next room.

"Yeah, I'd like to hear that," says Peacock. Friedman nods in agreement, spies a small electric heater in a corner of the room, switches it on, and props his chilly, stockinged feet on top of it.

The tape is rolling on the playback. The three musicians listen. A crescendo followed by a pause finds Giuffre with his arms raised, shaking both his hands and thrusting out his right foot, smiling broadly. The music ends jarringly at the point where the tape had run out.

"You sure learn a lot from hearing yourself back right away," Giuffre says to mutual nods.

Giuffre returns from the kitchen with three small glasses of beer, and the musicians unwind with small talk. "Hey, do you realize we are a West Coast trio?"

At a pause, Peacock begins to speak seriously and almost formally on the music: "You know, I have the feeling that the volume of this music creates a weight, regardless of which register you're playing in.

Ordinarily, the lower parts of the piano, say, are heavy, and the upper notes are light. But in this music I don't feel that at all. Here, loud in any register, high or low, is heavy. Quiet, high or low, is lightweight. Of course, I don't have the range of dynamics on bass that the other instruments have."

"Well," Giuffre contributes, "the bass in this music is definitely called upon to play three or four times as loud as in any other, and it usually takes a player a while to realize that."

"There was a very good thing that happened in our duo," Friedman says to Peacock. "When I played down, you went up high; when I played high, you went low; when I went slow, you moved faster. . . ."

"Fine," Giuffre says, "as long as it doesn't get monotonous or seem mechanical. Or as long as one man doesn't take over and dominate the music."

Peacock is back to Friedman's thought, saying:

"The point I wanted to bring out is that I can get presence—I can get the audience to hear me clearly —by playing low when you're high, high when you're low, by leaving holes, and so forth. But that in itself has nothing to do with the music necessarily. Then, I can play something that does fit musically but doesn't have presence and isn't heard. It's essentially my problem, I know, and not yours." He gestures toward Giuffre and Friedman.

"Also you are usually microphoned," says Friedman, "and here you're not. . . ."

"No, not in this music," Giuffre says, emphatically.

"I don't know whether *we're* playing too loud," he adds, pointing to himself and Friedman.

"No," Peacock decides, "the bass player has to hear how he is situated within the musical context and play accordingly."

The room holds a pause for a couple of beats, after which Giuffre speaks for the three of them: "Let's do some more." Peacock wiggles his eyebrows in assent. Friedman moves to the piano.

Giuffre is in the rear again to start the tape recorder. Friedman, a gleam in his eyes, slyly starts blocking out some chords. Peacock starts to walk along behind him. After about thirty seconds of this conventionality, the pianist is complaining, "I'm tired already."

Giuffre re-enters, saying, "Look, before we do the piece again, want to try playing something, just the two of you for a little bit? Want me to listen?"

Peacock turns to Friedman and says, "Let's play the duet." Immediately they go into the second part of *Trio in Flux*. Each of Friedman's crisp phrases swings its own way. And Peacock's musical logic carries its momentum in complement.

"I didn't notice any lack of presence that time," the bassist says at the end.

"I think you're right," Giuffre agrees. "But the piano has so many overtones in this room that they blotted you out sometimes. It was partly the room, partly the material, and partly the instrument. Now, after all this talk, let's do another tape."

They are into the piece. This time Giuffre has

moved from the piano's curve and stands behind Friedman's keyboard, in the midst of the group and its suspended sounds.

When each section of *Trio in Flux* is over, each player knows it almost intuitively, and all three turn to the next written part together. And there is never any doubt for a listener either when the group's free exploration of a section is over emotionally or musically.

The piece is finished, and Friedman says quietly, "That was sure a lot different from the first time."

Giuffre takes a step toward the recorder in the next room, commenting, "I think we did all the things we talked about doing."

RECORD NOTE

The development of the Trio's music can be heard on *"Thesis"* (Verve V-8395) and on the later *"Free Fall"* (Columbia CL 1964).

COMMENT
BY A LISTENER

The Tenacious Craft
of Horace Silver

Pianist and composer Horace Silver is often said
to have been the founder of a movement or a style, a
kind of return-to-roots on the part of modern jazzmen. The music—at first called funky (after an old
Anglo-Saxonism for smelly)—rediscovered, in the
blues and in contemporary Negro gospel music, important qualities that jazz reputedly had lost sight of
as it turned cool in the early Fifties and subsequently
froze stiff on the West Coast. The descriptive tags associated with funky jazz were *wail, groove, swing,
blow, cook, low-down*—almost all of them implying
passionate and uninhibited expression, and several of
them (for good reason, as we shall see) rescued from
the jazz argot of the Thirties.

However, soon after it had arrived, the funky style
became, through simplifications that amounted to a

grinding parody, a marketable commodity called "soul jazz." And before long soul jazz had had its day at the box office.

Nevertheless, funky jazz itself had reasserted fundamentals when they needed reasserting. For Silver it became a question of whether his work was done, his talent spent, in having rallied jazz to the initially just cause of the late Fifties. And the answer, it turns out, lies not only in his current work but in a review of his past.

Horace Silver doesn't come from "down home" at some Southern or Middle Western whistle stop, as his music might imply; to Horace Silver, down home is Norwalk, Connecticut. He was, at first, a tenor saxophonist, but a spinal condition forced him to undertake an instrument he could play sitting down. He first began to attract attention during 1950 and 1951 as player and composer for Stan Getz's small groups, and his piano was succinctly effective, bounding and rumbling away behind the tenor saxophonist. Getz's own stylistic roots are planted directly in the late Thirties, and so (if a bit less directly) are Silver's. Indeed, one's first estimate of Silver was apt to be that he sounded a bit like modernist Bud Powell imitating boogie-woogie man Pete Johnson. And Silver's own quintets, formed a few years later, were to suggest a cross between a 1937 swing band and a 1947 be-bop quintet. But the result was more than an ingenious hybrid.

Silver's impact on New York musicians was immediate, and for a while in the mid-Fifties he was everybody's pianist on record dates, particularly Miles Davis' pianist and Milt Jackson's. By 1955, Silver was a member of the Art Blakey Jazz Messengers. When that group recorded for Blue Note under Silver's name, the pianist's ideas began to emerge more fully, and a period of cooking and wailing in New York jazz was irrevocably at hand.

To some of Silver's followers, cooking and wailing and performing just about anything that encourages finger-snapping and head-shaking in an audience was about all there was to it. But Silver's music is carefully designed and frequently rehearsed, and the pianist's craftsmanship is constantly at work.

His most interesting early piece of writing is called *Hippy*. Its germ idea is also a little traditional two-bar riff. But instead of hypnotically repeating it over and over, as the jazz arrangers of the Thirties would have done, Silver developed it further into a continuous and delightful melody that bounces and swings along for a full eight bars, after the manner of modern jazz. And *Hippy* also has a secondary theme that echoes big-band brass figures. It is this sort of delightful synthesis of the Thirties and the Forties that characterizes Silver's best work.

Thus it seems inaccurate to class Silver with those of his followers who turned rigidly to gospel music and to a rather self-conscious emphasis on "soul." Silver's popular *The Preacher*—a leaping, shouting melody built on the structure of the barroom favorite *Show Me the Way to Go Home*—might even have been named as a kind of joke. And although *Sister*

Sadie has a faintly ecclesiastical title, the lady in question could have got her funkyness from dancing to swing bands as easily as from shouting gospel songs at a Holiness church.

Sister Sadie is quite a performance. It has the kind of sustained drive and surging swing that musicians are not supposed to be able to achieve in the cold afternoon atmosphere of a recording studio—or for that matter even in a jazz nightclub before about 1:30 A.M. For variety, *Sadie* has an effective secondary theme on which Silver makes his two horns (Blue Mitchell's trumpet and Junior Cook's tenor saxophone), plus ingenious complements from his own piano, sound almost exactly like the alternating brass and reed section riffing of a big band. Ordinarily, one may wonder why a musician would want to make a quintet sound like a big band, but with the results that Silver gets on *Sister Sadie* one is simply too awed and too admiring to bother with such points.

Another Silver piece called *Cookin' at the Continental* is a faster *tour de force* of the same kind of ingenuity of writing and energy of performance, and it is just about as successful as *Sadie*. One should also mention Silver's very interesting secondary theme or interlude on the piece he calls *Moonrays*, a striking combination of sophisticated lyricism and swing-period guttiness.

It has been said that several of Silver's quintet performances might be better if he had limited his horn men to about half the solo space he gave them. But that is to forget that Silver can be particularly ingenious and skillful in protecting a player against his own shortcomings or against the inevitable "off night" when his inspiration may be weak. Many a Horace Silver composition is written with a dense and constantly shifting obstacle course of chord changes. An improviser who courses through them properly may sound as if he were playing a great deal even when he may be playing very little.

Another aspect of Silver's career has been his special—perhaps curious—relationship to several trumpeters. He was in frequent attendance during Miles Davis' artistic rebirth in the middle Fifties. Kenny Dorham's energetic style matured while both he and Silver were members of the Blakey Messengers. And Art Farmer—not coincidentally, I feel sure—became an exceptionally fluent and cohesive lyricist while with Silver. Similarly, Silver's later horn, Blue Mitchell. That any player might gain in rhythmic firmness and dexterity from experience with Horace Silver should be obvious. But trumpeters seem to gain as melodists while pianist Silver chops and bounds away behind them.

Silver's shortcomings as a pianist in his early days were directly related to the fact that he could swing hard and had somewhat simplified the modern piano style. In the first place, he had trouble with slow tempos and ballads. And in the second, his melodic figures seemed to be choppy, discontinuous fragments, scurrying away from his barking left hand, one after another. Thus he set up a kind of pianistic ping-pong: left-hand chord/right-hand figure; left-hand chord/right-hand figure; left-hand chord/right-hand figure.

More recently Silver has had the commendable insight to make virtues of his pianistic shortcomings. The oddly titled piece *The St. Vitus Dance*, performed by a Silver trio of piano with bass and drums, is full of lushly romantic harmonies and shows that Silver can make almost any musical device sound naturally and unself-consciously earthy, and that his melodic improvising has reached a level of lyric continuity and design one might once have thought impossible.

In another trio piece, *Sweet Stuff*, Silver again uses somewhat fragmented right-hand figures. The tempo is slow, but *Sweet Stuff* is firmly unsentimental. And one gradually realizes that Silver is building, in heavy chords and spurts of melody, a kind of chant or incantation, and that he has turned what was once a discontinuity or choppiness into a cornerstone of his style.

Horace Silver's jazz is full of rhythms other than the usual 2/4, 4/4, or 6/4. He is also very proud of breaking through the clichés of thirty-two-bar popular song forms and their eight-bar substructures, to write phrases of, say, six bars in pieces of thirty-eight bars. But these are not so much innovations as they are acts of sound conservatism—they find fresh ways of presenting fundamentals. And the fundamentals of Silver's music come from his remarkably perceptive alliance of the Thirties and the Forties, from his conscientious craftsmanship, and from his compelling musical energy.

Genius, in the history of jazz, belongs to individual improvisers like Louis Armstrong, Charlie Parker, and Ornette Coleman, who periodically renew its basic musical language. It also belongs to men like Jelly Roll Morton, Duke Ellington, and Thelonious Monk, who give the music larger compositional synthesis and form.

But art cannot exist on genius alone. It must have inspired followers like Fletcher Henderson, Don Redman, Count Basie, and Roy Eldridge. Such men seem to come along when the music needs the impetus of their particular talents, but the best of them can survive that moment. And such a first-rate creative craftsman is Horace Silver.

RECORD NOTES

Silver's leadership of the Art Blakey Jazz Messengers is preserved on Blue Note 1518, with *Room 608*, *Hippy*, *The Preacher*, *Doodlin'*, etc.

Sister Sadie is on Blue Note 4017, as is *The St. Vitus Dance*. *Cookin' at the Continental*, *Sweet Stuff*, and *Mellow D* are on Blue Note 4008.

Silver is in the company of Miles Davis on *Walkin'* and *Blue 'n' Boogie* on Prestige 7076, and in the company of Milt Jackson on Prestige 7224. The presence of Art Farmer in a Silver quintet can be heard on Blue Note 1589, which includes *Moonrays*.

Silver's studio recordings being so exceptionally successful, perhaps Blue Note recorded its LP 4076 called "*Doin' the Thing*") "live" at the Village Gate nightclub only to prove that the Silver group can play as well in a club as it does in a recording studio.

Silver's Serenade is Blue Note 4131.

The Triumphant Decline
of Billie Holiday

There is one point of view which holds that feeling was all Billie Holiday had in her latter days—that her voice and her musicianship were gone and that one heard only a woman with a stark and compelling talent for dramatic recitative. There is another point of view which holds that Billie Holiday did not really exist in her later years, that after, say, 1950, there was only the husk of a reputation, that the real Billie Holiday was the spirited young jazz singer of the Thirties and the nightclub success of the Forties.

I am not so sure, for it seems to me that the Billie Holiday of the Fifties was not only a great dramatic performer, but an even greater jazz singer because she was a greater musician.

During the late Forties Billie Holiday briefly acquired a following among the sort of well-heeled night-

club patrons who had attended Helen Morgan or
Libby Holman and who a few years later were to
make Edith Piaf an American success. But Billie Holiday had a musicianship quite beyond that required of
a popular cabaret singer, and she had a perspective on
her material that could make the torch singers' weepy
laments sound like self-indulgent delusion.

Oddly, her musicianship had little to do with her
vocal equipment; her voice and her range were small
from the beginning. But the extremely personal quality of her sound, so arresting and even shocking the
first time one hears it, was absolutely appropriate to
every other aspect of her art. That was true in the
beginning and it remained true even as her voice thick-
ened and deteriorated, as untrained voices (and some
trained ones) are apt to do.

Her musicianship had to do partly with her sense of
time and rhythm, which could be perfect in the most
adverse circumstances and with flounderingly inept
accompaniment. It had to do with her superb ability
to sustain a song at any tempo that seemed to her
appropriate and in any mood that she chose. One
might suspect that her musicianship also had to do
with her restrained use of her vocal techniques, but
her sense of pace is perhaps a natural result of the fact
of her limited range—of her very lack of technical
equipment. On the other hand, many a capable pop
singer can boast of comparable equipment in rhythmic sureness and technical discipline. Billie Holiday's
essential musicianship lay where it should lie for a
great jazz artist, in her ability to make variations. An

excellent example is the one that André Hodeir has cited, her 1952 version of *These Foolish Things*. She retains the original song's best melodic phrases, but instinctively rejects its inferior ones, filling in with new melodic lines of her own that are more interesting and more appropriate. In her earlier version of *These Foolish Things* she had similarly spotted its inferior moments but she was still a bit intimidated by them, and rather than come up with new melodic phrases of her own she had used simple blues devices to avoid them. Thus, whatever happened to her voice over the years, her jazz musicianship increased.

Her musical instincts were so true that she would alter only slightly when slight alteration was all that was called for. In her opening to *The Man I Love* she raises one note, adds an accent, delays a phrase, and recomposes the original into something of her own.

On her very earliest records, made in 1933 with a studio orchestra led by Benny Goodman, she still used a few of the growly tricks of the "hot" singer of the late Twenties, of the young Ethel Waters for example. But by 1936, when she was recording on her own and also with Teddy Wilson's little studio-assembled groups, it had become perfectly clear who were her stylistic masters. She was frank about it herself: she said she liked Bessie Smith's power and Louis Armstrong's style. On *A Fine Romance* from 1936 she is clearly Armstrong's pupil, a fact even more in evidence on songs that they both recorded like *Pennies from Heaven, I Can't Give You Anything But Love,* or *When You're Smiling.*

It is a patent contradiction that the warm geniality of Louis Armstrong's vocal choruses could be appropriate in the stark emotional world of Billie Holiday, but it was not only his vocal choruses that had attracted her. She learned from his trumpet the deeper and more complex vehicle of his art; she took whatever aspects of that side of Louis Armstrong she needed and she made them her own. She was drawn to the greatest Armstrong, the Armstrong of 1929 to 1933, the majestic melodist poised above the beat, above his accompaniment, and above his material—but with his emotional roots planted firmly.

A striking case in point is Armstrong's 1933 version of *I Gotta Right to Sing the Blues* and the one Billie Holiday did six years later; whatever departures from the original she makes that are not her own, they echo Armstrong's trumpet passages on the piece as much as his vocal chorus.

Consider the way these early Billie Holiday records were made: Like the similar recordings of new pop material made by Henry "Red" Allen a few years before and by Fats Waller contemporaneously, the Holiday and Wilson records were primarily intended for sales to jukebox operators in urban Negro areas (these were Depression days and there weren't many people buying records for playing at home). The assemblage was strictly a last minute, pick-up affair, but the players usually came from the Basie, Henderson, Goodman, or Ellington orchestras. The repertory allowed for occasional standard tunes, but most often the players and the singer were handed the latest would-be "hits," uncritically selected, presented on publishers' "lead sheets" which offered the words for Miss Holiday and the melody notes plus some simple harmony for the players. They learned these songs, transformed them, worked up simple arrangements and effects, and committed them to wax.

Some of the dog tunes just couldn't be helped much, and the singer and the players did not always succeed. But brilliant success could come in the most unexpected ways. The idea that Billie Holiday could sing something called A *Sailboat in the Moonlight* (*And You*) to any effect except a ludicrous one may seem preposterous, yet she sang it beautifully, and tenor saxophonist Lester Young accompanied her in one of the great examples of jazz counterpoint on record.

Sometimes she transmuted her material by bold departure from it (*Without Your Love*); sometimes she treated a puerile song with such an implied sarcasm that its puerility never had a chance (*Getting Some Fun Out of Life*); and sometimes she could sing a song as if she half believed it—or at least as if she discerned the human truth its banal words pretended to be getting at (*If Dreams Come True*).

One should not leave these early recordings without some further praise for her accompanists—surely *Georgia on My Mind*, *Laughing at Life*, and *Easy to Love* would be good jazz recordings if only for Teddy Wilson's contribution to them. It has been said that Lester Young's was the closest musical temperament to her own, but I don't agree. The trumpeters on these records, for example, Buck Clayton and Roy Eldridge, had worked out personal styles under Armstrong's tutelage, as she had. Lester Young was an original and a precursor of the jazz to come, and in Billie and Lester, two jazz areas met in superb musical discourse.

Those who hold that the younger Billie Holiday was the best Billie Holiday hold with her 1939 version of *Yesterdays*, which comes from the period of her first "supper club" success. Hearing the way she transmutes its calculated nostalgia into human pathos one may agree, for the moment at least, that they are right. One price of her growing success was that she began to get more formal arrangements by larger groups on her recordings, but from this period comes one example of a great jazz singer doing an exceptional popular song, Billie Holiday's *Lover Man*, and it is surely some sort of tribute to the public taste that this one became a best-selling record.

After 1952 she was back to recording with small and relatively informal groups of jazz musicians, but the show was really all hers and in a way that it had never been before. Her musicianship—her ability to invent melodies, to vary them, to retain what was good as written or to retain what was good from her own earlier versions of the songs she re-recorded—was more highly developed than ever.

And her voice? It may well be that it deteriorated, but for me the disheveled edge of her sound comes from deeply suppressed tears, tears which she simply could not let go without the deeper self-pity she denied herself, suppressed tears upon which every emotion she undertook—from gaiety even to sadness—was imposed. No one could help her and she could not help herself; in that essential sense she was a tragic being.

But to say more is to go more deeply into her biography and that is something which, in speaking of Billie Holiday the singer, one should not do. Her life may have been personally tragic, but her art was always soundly histrionic, for she had the ability of a great actress to keep a personal distance from both her material and her performance of it and to imply a criticism of it.

Take 3 sat.

RECORD NOTES

Columbia's three-LP set, *"Billie Holiday: The Golden Years,"* includes the early version of *These Foolish Things, The Man I Love, A Fine Romance, Pennies from Heaven, I Can't Give You Anything But Love, When You're Smiling, Without Your Love, Getting Some Fun Out of Life,* and *If Dreams Come True.* Another Columbia compilation, *"Lady Day"* (CL 637), includes the Holiday-Lester Young collaborations on *Me, Myself and I* and *A Sailboat in the Moonlight.*

Mainstream 6000 has the first *Yesterdays* and *I Gotta Right to Sing the Blues.*

Lover Man is a part of Decca's *"The Billie Holiday Story"* (DXB-161).

The second and classic version of *These Foolish Things*

is on the Verve album, *"The Unforgettable Lady Day"* (MGV-8338-2). The set also preserves a 1946 concert, plus a good cross-section of her 1952–57 studio recordings.

Krupa Collected

Few Americans who are about to leave their thirties or have entered their forties could avoid having some idea of who Gene Krupa is or what he does. In the period when Benny Goodman's popularization of "swing" music brought jazz the largest audience it had ever had, Krupa was everyone's second enthusiasm; he was cheered by many, idolized by almost as many, and imitated by literally thousands of amateur drummers who hounded their parents for a drum set of their own. He has the claim to infame in jazz history that he established the long drum solo as standard practice, and, along with Goodman, his name is still a symbol for jazz music among the unhip.

Krupa's popularity was readily understandable. As a player, his enthusiasm for his work, his fellow musicians, and his audience is immediately and infectiously communicated and entirely generous. It is also superbly self-effacing, for behind the sweaty, flashy showmanship, there is always emotional and personal honesty.

His heritage is authentic, consisting (I would say) of Baby Dodds, Zutty Singleton, and Chick Webb. Krupa also had a dedication to his craft that kept him practicing and constantly polishing and expanding his techniques.

However, at the same time that Gene Krupa was winning the popularity polls, Sidney Catlett, Jo Jones, Dave Tough, and Jimmy Crawford were also practicing jazz drummers, and the realization that this is so is apt to bring one up short and make one ask a few questions.

Much as one would not accuse Krupa of calculated grandstanding, one would not accuse him of subtlety. He knows when to switch from snare to cymbals and when to switch from sticks to brushes (play those figures with the trumpets; softer now, the pianist is soloing!) and yet his switches always seem mechanical and obvious, no matter how just. And he is sometimes loud, when drums, somewhat in the manner of proper Victorian children, are better sensed than heard. (His heavy-handed accents behind Goodman and Teddy Wilson on the Quartet's *The Man I Love* seem to me models of insensitivity to melody and mood.)

More crucial is his rhythm. Not to argue with his evenness or steadiness, but to say that Krupa is so often just an unmeasureable but detectable shade ahead of things, enough ahead to preclude that secret but mandatory jazz quality called "swing." The effect is an edginess, a compulsion that may seem to an auditor rather like a percussive nervousness. It could not be unfair to compare Krupa to his fellow Chicagoans of a similar heritage, and in such a comparison both George Wettling and, certainly, Dave Tough come off as players with more swing than Krupa. Similarly Krupa's own stylistic successor, Buddy Rich, albeit a sometimes overbearing drummer, can swing.

Krupa was the first of many famous Goodman sidemen to leave him, departing in 1938 to form his own band. It was actually the first of two Krupa bands; the second came in the postwar years 1945–49, and its arrangers and sidemen reflected the new jazz, then (alas!) called "be-bop." Columbia has collected thirty-two titles by both these groups in a two-LP set, *"Drummin' Man"* (C2L 29).

One is struck in the Columbia set by Krupa's alertness to the more musical aspects of the jazz being played during any period. We begin with his theme, *Apurksody*, which is an attempt at an Ellington pastiche. And we end with *Lemon Drop*, a very good Charlie Parker-inspired melody. In between we hear, for example, Chappie Willett's *Rhythm Jam* out of Don Redman–Fletcher Henderson, and Gerry Mulligan's *Disc Jockey Jump* and Eddie Finkle's *Calling Dr. Gillespie*, both out of Parker–Gillespie. Yet so much of this music is delivered on the level of "novelty tunes," and this is not a question of the selections included in the Columbia set, for one would have only a few quibbles over what is left out of the complete Krupa discography. What we have is what we must have: the inane lyrics on (*He's That*) *Drummin'*

Man, Drum Boogie, Bolero at the Savoy, Gene's Boogie. Even *Lemon Drop* is done as a scatbop vocal, one of many in the set. (But the first scat vocal is a good one, a bit of gleeful nonsense from Leo Watson, called *Tutti Frutti.*) And, among other things, there are the current hits and would-be hits of yesteryear such as *Massachusetts* and *Skylark.*

I seem to be saying that what we have here is largely a collection of period pieces 1938–1949, nostalgic perhaps and not yet old enough to be quaint. Largely, yes, but not entirely.

Searing above the opening measures of *Bolero at the Savoy* is the trumpet of Roy Eldridge, and there is nothing nostalgic or quaint about its kind of personal vitality. Eldridge was a member of Krupa's orchestra during his peak years, and he was, surely, the most individually developed bravura jazz trumpeter between Louis Armstrong and Dizzy Gillespie. Many of his performances here are also among the novelties and hits: besides the *Bolero,* he plays on *Massachusetts, Skylark,* and his own largely vocal piece *Knock Me a Kiss.* Still, *Let Me Off Uptown* (which became a hit for Krupa, Anita O'Day, and Eldridge) does have a fine, shouting trumpet chorus —full of oh-how-imitated ideas, one realizes on hearing it again. Then there are his two instrumental showpieces, *Rockin' Chair* and *After You've Gone.* Surely between Armstrong's 1933 *I Gotta Right to Sing the Blues* and Dizzy Gillespie's 1945 *I Can't Get Started,* there is hardly a ballad by any jazz trumpeter but Eldridge's *Rockin' Chair.* And surely there are no trumpeter's fast virtuoso pieces between Armstrong's *Ding Dong Daddy* and Gillespie's *Dizzy Atmosphere* like Eldridge's *After You've Gone*. And just as surely, Gillespie did not "supplant" Eldridge—any more than Eldridge supplanted Armstrong.

I will not insult Roy Eldridge by saying that his presence alone makes the whole Columbia set worth its price. I don't know what excellence costs. I will say that he is one of those players whose work affirms jazz as a player's art, and whose recordings also show that what is invented on the spur of the moment can survive the years.

Notes on Four Pianists

George Shearing

A few years ago, pianist George Shearing said that "Lennie [Tristano] could never be happy compromising, as I am doing." Shearing's frankness and lack of delusion are admirable to be sure. What he was and is doing is popularizing modern jazz to a widespread success.

I am not absolutely sure that musical popularizers are a reviewer's business. They do introduce large numbers of people to a musical style—at least so I am told. But for every listener who moves on, hundreds of others stay with the popularizer; one of the originators of modern jazz, Dizzy Gillespie, had a good audience before Shearing arrived, but Shearing has a larger audience than Gillespie has or probably ever will have. In any case, popularizers always appear and are always going to appear.

However, there are popularizers and popularizers. One of Benny Goodman's functions was to spread a music that Fletcher Henderson had evolved several years before and do the same for some of Count Basie's pieces as well. Goodman contributed more than merely that, to be sure, but his treatment of Henderson's style involved no particular compromise or dilution.

I suppose that if popularizers become a constant preoccupation, a reviewer will be wasting a great deal of time. And, at worst, he may end up making them the objects of a kind of snobbish abuse. On the other hand, a reviewer probably should discuss them from time to time to describe what he feels they are up to and to say how much compromise and dilution he hears in their work.

I begin with Shearing because Capitol has issued a kind of summary album of his career, *"The Best of George Shearing"* (T 2104; stereo ST 2104). As a pianist, Shearing is able and fluent, although as a jazz-man he has occasional problems with phrasing and swing. More important, he is capable of a lot more inventiveness than he usually offers. And it seems to me that his basic compromise is to play as if he were not really emotionally involved with what he is doing, even when he allows himself to do something musical.

His group's approach comes partly from its instrumentation (piano, vibraharp, guitar, plus bass and drums), and the formula usually involves an opening theme-statement by the three melody instruments.

The tone is terribly chic and usually employs some rather gimmicky and mechanical rhythmic displacements. Then we get a chorus from Shearing of single-note treble lines, followed by another chorus of locked-hands block chording. Finally, a repeat of the first chorus.

The selections in the album are usually laid out in that manner, although a few supplement it with a string section, or some "Latin" percussion, or the applause of a "live" audience.

To be more specific, *Lullaby of Birdland*, which has some rather abruptly chunky work by the rhythm section, involves no solos except some bass breaks, and *You Stepped Out of a Dream*, with a conga drummer added, involves no solos at all. *September in the Rain* has an opening chorus with some trite embellishments from the pianist, moves on to a good modernish piano variation played rather tepidly, then to some mechanical block-chording. On *You Don't Know What Love Means*, Shearing offers a tinkly, obvious, cocktail-style variation. The quintet turns Lester Young's movingly ironic blues, *Jumpin' with Symphony Sid*, into a lightweight ditty, and Shearing plays four frothy choruses that nevertheless are very well organized. On *Dream*, Shearing delivers an unexpected solo in a Teddy Wilson style; on *East of the Sun* he does capable Oscar Peterson. *Roses in Picardy* has piano notes and runs, but no real ideas. So does *September Song*, along with some writing for strings that is so trite as to be funny. *Early Autumn* has a good enough half-chorus played, once again, with tinkling shallowness. A version of *Honeysuckle Rose* is done in a sort of pseudo-earthy style, with lots of blue notes and a boogie-woogie bass figure.

There is one exceptional performance: an extended reading of *Little White Lies*, with real group swing, very good drumming, good solos by guitar and vibes, and Shearing showing the basic debt of his modern style: simplified Bud Powell.

Oscar Peterson

Popular art, we are told, finds its chief effect in an emotional immediacy. On that basis there can be no doubt of the effectiveness of Oscar Peterson as a popular artist. And it does not take much reflection in tranquillity to discern Peterson's virtues nor the pleasures to be found in his playing. They are engagingly obvious—perhaps too obvious to need talking about. At least they are obvious enough so that his admirers are usually surprised to discover that there are some who have reservations about his playing.

There are two inevitable words in any talk about Oscar Peterson: *technique* and *swing*. Perhaps neither is the *mot juste*. There can be no question about the finger dexterity of Peterson's piano, certainly; he can handle the shortest notes and the fastest tempos. There are recorded versions of *Indiana* and *Elevation* (Verve V-8482) (to take two from dozens of possible examples) that are very fast and on which Peterson offers a plentitude of notes with a rhythmic exactness and sureness that only a few jazz pianists could equal.

But technique is as technique does. If a reference to musical technique also implies musical expressiveness, then it might be better to say that what Peterson has is facility. Quite often his dexterity seems to be a detriment. He cannot resist, it seems, obvious triplets, scales, and arpeggio runs as they occur to him, and time and again he will interrupt the perfectly respectable musical structure he has been building to run off such pianistic platitudes.

Nor, it seems, can Peterson resist a jazz cliché. He even interrupts the theme statement of so delicately rendered a line as Clifford Brown's *Joy Spring* (an almost perfectly titled piece, by the way) (Verve V-8482) with a hoary and inappropriate riff. One might almost say that Peterson's melodic vocabulary is a stockpile of clichés, that he seems to know every stock riff and lick in the history of jazz. Further, his improvisations frequently just string them together. One has the feeling that Peterson will eventually work every one of them into every piece he plays, regardless of tempo, mood, or any other consideration; it will simply be a matter of his going on long enough to get them all in.

Possibly the biggest cliché in Peterson's style is his constant preoccupation with the blue notes. Miles Davis has said that he sounds as if he had to *learn* to play the blues. He certainly sounds as if he were out to prove he had learned to, for on nearly every piece he plays *at* the blues. And with Peterson these plaintively expressive musical resources often lose their effect, sometimes within less than two choruses, since he uses them so constantly and indiscreetly.

There could probably be no more succinct contrast to such cliché-mongering than the presence of bassist Ray Brown in Peterson's group. Brown's virtues are many—his sound, his excellent and sympathetic swing, his joyous and natural commitment to the act of playing. His solos (take the ones on *Kadota's Blues* or *Tricrotism* on Verve V-8480 or his more celebrated variations on *How High the Moon* on Verve V-8024) do contain some stock effects, and they prove that there is nothing innately wrong with stock effects. Brown uses them as parts of a personally developed musical context; he grasps the meaning of these traditional and durable ideas, and as he uses them we inevitably see them in a different light and glimpse the sound basis for their durability. All of which is quite a different matter from glibly piling up such phrases, one on another.

The question of Peterson's swing is perhaps similar. If there were some mechanical means for measuring swing, Peterson might get a score of 100 per cent. And there can be no question that he is a rhythmically engaging player. Peterson seems to know everything there is to know about swing—except perhaps its essence, its musical meaning. For, as he bounces along, Oscar Peterson never seems to have the creative momentum in his lines that is perhaps the real *raison d'être* for swing.

I have spoken of his fast tempos, and I should also

compliment his slow ones, for Peterson has a range in tempos that few jazzmen can duplicate. He seems to be able to play, unembarrassed, with the same bounce and cleanness, fairly slow, medium, and fast.

Peterson is obviously indebted to the Nat Cole of the Forties (when Cole was a jazz pianist) and to Art Tatum. Some may feel that Peterson's facility and sophistication allow him to fill out ideas that Cole merely suggested. But Nat Cole had a sense of melodic order and, though one might question his taste in melodic ideas, his constructions often had a relatively sustained design. By comparison Peterson seems to think only from one two-bar riff to the next.

At slow tempos Peterson does use a directly Tatumesque manner—a recorded performance of *Ill Wind* (Verve V-8480) is an example. Whatever one's final opinion of Tatum, there is a wonderful sense of pianistic adventure and an arresting harmonic imagination in his playing. Peterson's pastiche seems to me mechanical. His heavier touch seems inappropriate to such a style, and his monotony in dynamics is dramatized in such moods.

With such a heritage, Peterson would seem to belong to the Thirties and, for all his harmonic sophistication, he does. His rhythmic sense, his manner of phrasing, is the clue to that, of course, and with his facility a kind of rococo version of Thirties jazz piano is probably inevitable. For all his dexterity, his phrasing (the way he *thinks* rhythmically) is so deeply rooted in the earlier period that when he occasionally reaches for a Parkeresque double-timing (as on the aforementioned *Joy Spring*, for example) he seems a bit strained and uncomfortable. He has recorded with almost every major player from the Thirties, and on occasion he has shown commendable sympathy for their work. One thinks particularly of his accompaniments to Roy Eldridge: he begins with the sparsest and simplest textures which gradually build and buoy up the trumpeter, inspiring him to a third, perhaps a fourth improvised variation. On the other hand, on the LP called *"Soulville"* (Verve V-8274) he glibly accompanies Ben Webster, and spells him in solo, with an almost constant rattling of blue notes and tired riffs. Under the circumstances, the level of sustained inspiration Webster shows on that LP seems to me a marvel of marvels.

I began by quoting the dictum about the immediacy of popular art. (But is not Beethoven emotionally immediate?) Surely anyone who has watched early Chaplin will question that criterion, for obviously the best popular art refutes it. So also will anyone who has heard Armstrong or Ellington, Parker or Monk. Jazz long ago showed that its best players could provide a more durable aesthetic experience.

Ahmad Jamal

Pianist Ahmad Jamal is a success: he has several best-selling LPs, a supper-club following (which otherwise shows little interest in jazz), and several direct imitators. He has also received the deeper compliment

of having admittedly affected the work of an important jazzman. His success should surprise no one, and
his effect on Miles Davis should prove (if proof were
needed) that good art can be influenced by bad.

Clearly, Davis responds to some of Jamal's interesting harmonic substitutions and the very light and
impeccably accurate rhythmic pulse of Jamal's trio,
particularly in the support he got from his bassist, the
late Israel Crosby, and from his drummer, Vernell
Fournier. Further, Jamal has the same interest in
openness of melody, space, and fleeting silence that
Davis does. But for the trumpeter these qualities can
be aspects of haunting lyric economy. For Jamal they
seem a kind of crowd-titillating stunt-work. Indeed, in
a recital such as *"Ahmad Jamal at the Blackhawk"*
(Argo 703/S), recorded in a San Francisco nightclub,
it appears that Jamal's real instrument is not the piano
at all, but his audience. On some numbers, he will
virtually sit things out for a chorus, with only some
carefully worked out rhapsodic harmonies by his left
hand or coy tinklings by his right. After that, a few
bombastic block chords by both hands, delivered
forte, will absolutely lay them in the aisles. And unless
you have heard Ahmad Jamal blatantly telegraph the
climax of a piece, or beg applause en route with an
obvious arpeggio run which he drops insinuatingly on
the crowd after he has been coasting along on the
graceful momentum of Crosby and Fournier, then
you have missed a nearly definitive musical bombast.
The set in question includes slow and medium standards—Jamal this time seems to favor Richard Rod-

gers and Jimmy Van Heusen especially—and a blues by Jamal which is performed with a kind of chi-chi sophistication one might have thought impossible within that basic jazz form.

Dave Brubeck

"The Dave Brubeck Quartet at Carnegie Hall" (Columbia C2L-26/C2S-826) is the nearly self-explanatory title of a two-record set recorded by Brubeck, piano; Paul Desmond, alto saxophone; Gene Wright, bass; and Joe Morello, drums. The jacket notes add that, although the sequence of the program is slightly rearranged for LP, we hear the concert intact, with no editing and no surreptitious retakes (as is sometimes the case with "live" recording) done later in a recording studio. Judging from the bits of audience response heard here and there, the evening was a decided public success. Musically, it juxtaposed improvisation that is either highly successful or so decidedly faulty as to border on amateurishness. And most of the faults are the leader's.

As exhibited on his rephrasing of the familiar *Pennies From Heaven*, Dave Brubeck's idea of jazz rhythm resembles nothing so much as the awkwardly static fingering of a fraternity house pianist. Our example is not isolated, for he has the same kind of trouble with phrasing the *St. Louis Blues*, and by the time we get to his own piece, *It's A Raggy Waltz*, he sounds like an automaton, pounding away and managing somehow to keep the tempo, although his mainspring is rapidly running down. The crowd, one might note, is audibly enthralled by the spectacle.

Alas for a man with such rigid and static rhythmic limitations, Brubeck's approach to a solo is largely percussive. On the aforementioned *St. Louis Blues*, on *Blue Rondo à la Turk*, on *For All We Know*, he rummages through one cliché lick after another (big-band riffs, borrowings from Basie and Garner, even cocktail rhapsodizings) in structureless episodes whose monotony his occasional harmonic sophistications and modulations merely enhance. It takes a subtle rhythmic master (a Basie, a Monk, even a Horace Silver) with a refined sense of architectonics to play this kind of jazz piano. Brubeck, it seems to me, comes very close to simple-mindedness. And when he does undertake ideas that are more melodic they are apt to be virtuosic arrays of eighths and sixteenths (there are handy examples on *Bossa Nova U.S.A.*) in which his fingering fails him badly.

Under the circumstances, Brubeck's penchant for odd "experimental" meters (*Eleven Four*, *Take Five*, the *Rondo*, the *Waltz*) only dramatizes his rhythmic shortcomings. Happily, these are sometimes dropped after a first chorus or played *ostinato* in such a way that Desmond can glide over them, paying only slight heed.

Desmond, Wright, and Morello, happily, go their own way, except for fleeting and vain efforts on Morello's part to lead the leader. The momentum and swing generated on *King for a Day*, largely given over to Wright, is nothing short of a marvel of contrast.

And it is decidedly to Brubeck's credit that his accompaniments stay out of Desmond's way, for Desmond, nearly always an inventive melodist, was in excellent form. His solos—especially those on *Pennies from Heaven, St. Louis Blues,* and *Southern Scene* (a Brubeck compositional pastiche of the sort he does very well)—are full of ideas and wit, and they are all well designed. Indeed, they seem among the best he has recorded.

As I say, there are clear indications from the audience throughout the LP that Brubeck's popularity continues—and that popularity has held up, unabated, for almost ten years and survived several subsequent fads. His fame is also so curiously widespread that many people with only a nodding acquaintance with jazz think of him as both academically disciplined and experimentally daring. It seems to me that he is neither. But there is, I suppose, a kind of reassuring, "nice guy" quality in his genially unself-conscious pounding, and his playing does make a pleasant, undemanding companion. Desmond in his way is undemanding too. But he is still water, and he runs deep.

"The New Thing" in Jazz

As things go in jazz, twenty years is a long time. And for twenty years jazz was dominated by the musical language introduced by saxophonist Charlie ("Bird") Parker and trumpeter Dizzy Gillespie. This music was rather unfortunately called "be-bop" when it first found a following and it came—more fortunately—to be known as "modern jazz." Not too long ago the music of Gillespie and Parker produced shock and outrage, even to some avid followers of jazz, but today popularized versions of it are commonplace. Almost every Sunday the featured comedian on the Ed Sullivan show used to run off the stage to a little melody that is really a simplified version of an old Gillespie piece. And one TV comedy series has used a saxophone theme that is clearly a watering down of Charlie Parker's style.

In the 1960s a different kind of jazz emerged and once again its striking departures from the jazz that went before it produced outraged protest in some parts of the jazz world. For lack of a better name, some call this music "free-form jazz" or "the new thing"; others jokingly label it "space music"; with occasional accuracy it has been called "atonal jazz." Whatever it is called, practically everyone agrees that one of the leading figures involved is the saxophonist Ornette Coleman. In the late 1950s, composer and pianist John Lewis put down a reaction to Coleman's music which still describes some of the excitement of what is happening today:

There are two young people I met in California—an alto player named Ornette Coleman and a trumpet player named Don Cherry. I've never heard anything like them before. Ornette is the driving force of the two. . . . They play together like I've never heard anybody play together. It's not like any ensemble that I have ever heard, and I can't figure out what it's all about yet. Ornette is, in a sense, an extension of Charlie Parker and the first I've heard. This is the real need . . . to extend the ideas of Bird until they are not playing an imitation but actually something new. I think that they may have come up with something, not perfect yet, and still in the early stages, but nevertheless very fresh and interesting

Dizzy Gillespie has said that he, Thelonious Monk, and the others used to work out difficult chord progressions deliberately, to confuse the amateurs and keep them out of the experimental jam sessions that led to be-bop and modern jazz. A young musician said more recently, "We keep changing the tempo and the key and leaving out the chords altogether when we play so those damned be-boppers won't try to sit in with us." He didn't mean Gillespie or anyone like him, of course. But his statement is a reflection of the fact that many young players in jazz no longer find musical challenge in the language that Gillespie and Charlie Parker provided, and that many of the younger men who play their style play it in a derivative, mechanical, and conventional manner. Even the most searching and sincere players often seem so boxed in by the preset structures that they may appear to be running around like rats caught in a harmonic maze.

There were rumblings of change before it came. Bassist Charlie Mingus saw the coming deadlock and often shouted to his players to "stop copying Bird." Another evidence was the fact that men were looking to Monk for guidance. A third came about when Miles Davis herded his men—saxophonists John Coltrane and Julian ("Cannonball") Adderley and pianist Bill Evans —into a studio to make a record called *Kind of Blue*. Instead of improvising on the usual preset chord patterns, Davis required his men to make up their melodies from scales and modes which he assigned them on the spot, and let the harmonies fall where they may.

Meanwhile other musicians were experimenting with freer jazz forms. One was a young pianist named Paul Bley, another a pianist-composer named Cecil Taylor. Then in 1959 Ornette Coleman came to New

York. Charlie Mingus employed a reed man named Eric Dolphy. The composer George Russell formed a sextet. Even Jimmy Giuffre, decidedly from another generation, has been attracted to this new jazz and has used Bley in his trio.

Musicians working on "the new thing" were soon turning up almost daily in New York, and the players who are already known rattled off the names of other and yet unknown players with ease. Some of those who have been heard are good, some are not, some are merely faking—for "free" music may invite faking at this stage. At least one man is potentially a popularizer of the style. For a sympathetic listener, some of these men can create a whole new sensibility.

One is the pianist Cecil Taylor, who was academically trained at both the New York College of Music and the New England Conservatory. His playing clearly shows a knowledge of the classical composers of this century: Bartok, Stravinsky, Schönberg, and others. However, he is also aware of the jazz tradition and just as clearly displays familiarity with Ellington and Monk. But Taylor is a starkly emotional performer who does not often talk about his work. He may say that he hopes his playing speaks for itself and, if pressed further, that he plays to give people pleasure.

Ornette Coleman came to a new jazz by a very different route from Taylor's, and he plays it differently. A slight, soft-spoken, self-taught young man from Fort Worth, Coleman will talk about his music at length to anyone who is really interested, describing what he is doing modestly, candidly, in his own highly intuitive and sometimes cryptic way. Coleman heard the jazz of the Thirties played around him when he was growing up and he absorbed the work of Parker and Gillespie from records. He studied harmony from the stray books that were available. Soon he began writing his own pieces down in a personal style of notation that still gives other players trouble. By the late Forties, he was playing a style that some are still attacking as out of tune and in ignorance of harmony.

One probably significant fact is that Coleman used his sister's piano book for study. It was in C, whereas Coleman's alto saxophone was, of course, in E flat. This happy accident may have set him on his path, but the point is that he heard relationships when only an avant-garde classicist would have agreed with him. He later worked out his ideas on tenor saxophone, too. He hit on his general direction in terms of jazz and with no influence from classicism—and no academic snobbery about "improving jazz."

His idea, as he puts it, is "once the technical basis is understood, to be as free as possible. Not to play the framework, but to play the music itself."

Coleman's first jobs were with the small "rhythm and blues" groups that flourished throughout the South—and still do—the more honorable progenitors of the rock-and-roll style. Hostility to him ran high in most of the ensembles—he was thrown out of one for "trying to make a be-bopper" out of the other saxophonist in the group, and it got so that another leader was paying him not to play.

Stranded in Los Angeles for the second time, still kept from playing at jam sessions by musicians who accused him of musical ignorance, he was nevertheless presented as a potential composer to a record producer named Lester Koenig by the bassist Red Mitchell. But Coleman protested that he had no scores and he couldn't play his music on the piano. Instead he began performing *a cappella* on his saxophone and then Koenig wanted Coleman as well as his pieces.

Gradually things began to happen to him—help from John Lewis, a contract with Nesuhi Ertegun of Atlantic Records in New York—and by the fall of 1959 he had opened at the Five Spot in New York's lower east side with his own quartet. Coleman was soon packing the house, attracting reporters (some of them intrigued by the largely extrinsic fact that he then played an inexpensive plastic alto sax), and pulling in the intelligentsia—including a delighted Leonard Bernstein, an enthralled Marc Blitzstein, an approving Virgil Thomson, and an unsettled Kenneth Tynan ("They've gone too far!").

The lay listener should actually have far less initial trouble with Ornette Coleman's music than a musician whose ear searches automatically for the harmonic chord changes on which he expects jazz variations to be built. (Most musicians however agree that his writing can be superb. As one of them put it,

"Those themes sound so fresh and beautiful. Then they start to blow and it's—Cape Canaveral!") As for Coleman, he says, "If I am going to play on chords, I might as well write out my solo," and, "I think a theme should set up a musical direction and a pitch for the solo."

Coleman's variations may, in fact, be made on any of several elements of any given theme. The soloist's job becomes a free invention based on the general musical, rhythmic, or emotional areas that a theme suggests; he will usually play "modally," that is, within the key of the piece, but he will occasionally move out of it in a momentary atonality. The listener who says "he sounds like someone laughing, talking, and crying" is having the soundest sort of response. There is nothing really inaccessible about the *emotional* variations on Coleman recordings like *The Blessing*, the ironic *Tears Inside*, *Lorraine* (a memorial to pianist Lorraine Geller), *Lonely Woman*, or *Peace*, and most of the titles speak for themselves. And the rhythmic variations on *Ramblin'* (called by one man "a jazz version of hillbilly music") bring spontaneous responses from all sorts of audiences.

The role of the rhythm section in Coleman's group is almost reversed from previous jazz styles. Instead of the soloist following the rhythmic patterns set by the drummer and bass player, these musicians follow the soloist—or attempt to. This change is not as revolutionary as it might appear. It is often said that the appeal of older jazz is rhythmic and that the dixieland fan is responding to rhythm. But the rhythmic progress made in the history of jazz is enormous. Think of it: In 1930 a bassist, a guitarist, a pianist's left hand, a drummer's right foot and both his hands, would all be thumping away at timekeeping. Today only the string bass and perhaps the drummer's right hand on a cymbal will be playing the basic 1-2-3-4, 1-2-3-4. Meanwhile, the melodies themselves have evolved with far more rhythmic excitement and complexity.

Coleman wants even more rhythmic freedom and wants the drummer to play a kind of percussive part *within* the music rather than merely "accompanying" it. He told Nat Hentoff, "Rhythm patterns should be more or less like natural breathing patterns. I would like the rhythm section to be as free as I am trying to get, but very few players, rhythm or horns, can do this yet. Thelonious Monk can. He sometimes plays one note, and because he plays it in exactly the right pitch, he carries more music in it than if he filled out the chord. I'd say Monk has the most complete harmonic ear in jazz. Bird had the best diatonic ear."

Coleman's innovations are basically simple, inevitable, and authentic extensions of the jazz tradition— but they seem so only because his sublime stubbornness has made them. He has an eloquent answer to those who accuse him of inciting aesthetic chaos: "No. When I found out I could make mistakes, then I knew I was onto something."

His most far-reaching effort yet, called *Free Jazz*, took place in a recording studio. This is a continuous free improvisation by a "double" quartet—Coleman and the late Eric Dolphy, reeds; Cherry and Freddie

Hubbard, trumpets; Charlie Haden and the late Scott
La Faro, basses; Ed Blackwell and Billy Higgins,
drums. The only patterns followed were a series of
brief ensemble themes spaced so as to propel each
soloist in turn. The rest is entirely unpremeditated,
sometimes collective, improvising. And when they
were finished the performance had lasted over thirty-
eight minutes, long enough to fill both sides of an LP.
It is a strong experience and the section with dual
improvising by the two bass players is especially remarkable.

For all his willingness to discuss it, Coleman's
music is largely a matter of doing, of playing, of
testing ideas. The composer George Russell differs
from Coleman in that he has a theory to offer. Russell's career goes back to the first successes of modern
jazz; he wrote for the Gillespie band and for Parker.
He later evolved a theory of jazz "pantonality" based
on the Lydian mode, and several jazzmen have studied
with him. Whether his rationale is finally successful
for the "new" jazz, it has helped him find a renewed
career as leader of an advanced sextet.

Some "new thing" music is reactionary: players
know as much about Rex Stewart's trumpet style of
the Thirties as about Dizzy Gillespie's, and groups
may abandon "modern" jazz themes and actually play
familiar lines like *Honeysuckle Rose* or *Somebody
Loves Me*. The soloist changes tempos and key at will,
the accompanists follow. Players like pianist Paul
Bley and saxophonist Eric Dolphy began as virtuoso modern jazzmen and pushed things a bit fur-

ther. Bley has become a gentle lyricist. Dolphy was a nearly ferocious technician, whose style lay somewhere between Ornette Coleman's and that of an advanced and generally accepted modernist like John Coltrane. Dolphy readily acknowledged that Coleman "taught me a direction."

Ornette Coleman's music is an exhilarating move in an inevitable direction for jazz. The most telling evidence of his importance is that he has introduced new ideas of rhythm and his melodies involve new ways of phrasing. Parker's way of phrasing still clung to the improvising of Dolphy and several others. But like Parker, and like Armstrong before him, Coleman is developing a really new sensibility from a new rhythmic basis. When Charlie Mingus said of him that he sounded like "a million toned bongos" he went directly to the point. And jazz history clearly shows that anyone who tries to change jazz harmonically without revising his rhythms and phrasing inevitably risks either a bloodless affectation of meaningless sound patterns or pointless showers of technique.

Ornette Coleman gets the same kind of extreme reactions both within the jazz milieu and outside that any radical innovator must expect. Like Monk before him, he is both praised and called a kind of fake—among all the men mentioned in this survey of "the new thing," Coleman is the one whose work still remains "controversial." And this is natural, for his music takes the biggest step away from established convention into a real renewal of jazz.

RECORD NOTES

The Miles Davis *"Kind of Blue"* session with John Coltrane is on Columbia CL 1355. Coltrane's *"Crescent"* is on Impulse A-66.

Ornette Coleman's first LP was Contemporary 3551 and it includes *The Blessing; Tears Inside* and *Lorraine* are on Contemporary 3569. *Lonely Woman, Congeniality,* and *Peace* are on Atlantic 1317; *Ramblin'* and *The Face of the Bass* on Atlantic 1327; *Free Jazz,* for the double quartet, is Atlantic 1367.

Coleman's trumpet and violin work on the Blue Note albums *"At the Golden Circle"* (4224 and 4225) is only functionally effective, but his alto is also present, and the sets can be recommended for the remarkable developments they indicate in his music.

Perhaps the best introduction to Eric Dolphy's work is *"Last Date,"* Limelight LS 86013. A more adventurous Dolphy can be heard on Prestige 7294 and 7334.

INDEX

Related Quality Paperback Books from Da Capo Press

The Art of Jazz:
From Ragtime to Bebop
  Edited by Martin Williams

Django Reinhardt
  by Charles Delaunay

Blues Who's Who
  by Sheldon Harris

Music is My Mistress
  by Duke Ellington

Bird:
The Legend of Charlie Parker
  Edited by Robert Reisner

The Jazz Life
  by Nat Hentoff

Live At The Village Vanguard
  by Max Gordon

New York Notes:
A Journal of Jazz
in the Seventies
  by Whitney Balliett

. . . available at your bookstore